THE VISUAL DANCE

Creating Spectacular Quilts

Joen Wolfrom

C&T PUBLISHING

The Visual Dance—Creating Spectacular Quilts
©1995 Joen Wolfrom

Front Cover: *Feuerfacetten mit 2 Papageien* (Fire Facettes with
Two Parrots) by Erika Odemer, Munich, Germany, 1990.
Back Cover: *Hot August Night* by JoenWolfrom

Editor: Louise Owens Townsend, Pleasant Hill, California
Copy Editor: Judith M. Moretz, Pleasant Hill, California
Technical Editor: Joyce Engels Lytle, San Ramon, California
Design & Art Director: Bobbi Sloan Design, Berkeley, California
Hand-drawn Illustrations: Kathryn Darnell, East Lansing, Michigan
Computer-generated Illustrations: Rose Sheifer and Janet White,
Walnut Creek, California
Color Illustrations in Chapter Four:
Judith Buskirk, Gig Harbor, Washington

Photographer: Ken Wagner (unless otherwise noted),
Wagner Photo Lab, 1100 East Union I-D, Seattle, Washington 98122

Published by C&T Publishing, P.O. Box 1456,
Lafayette, California 94549

ISBN: 0-914881-93-0

Library of Congress Cataloging-in-Publication Data

Wolfrom, Joen.
    The visual dance—creating spectacular quilts / Joen Wolfrom
        p.   cm.
    Includes bibliographical references.
    ISBN: 0-914881-93-0
    1. Quilting. 2. Quilting—Patterns. 3. Color in textile crafts.
I. Title.
TT835.W647 1995
746.46—dc20   94-44610
                                      CIP

Liquitex is a registered trademark of Binney & Smith.

Printed in Hong Kong

10   9   8   7   6   5   4   3   2   1

Table of Contents

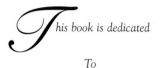

his book is dedicated

To
Connie, Bob, Jennie, Dan, and Linda Snell—
Sharing more than two decades of life together on the Bluff
has brought joy, love, unbelievable experiences,
and fond memories to two families
who have lived in close harmony with one another.
May the future give each of you many years of happiness
in your new adventures.
I shall dearly miss you all.

To
Diane Beaumont, Judy Buskirk, Roberta Palo,
Grania McElligott, Janice Richards,
Elly Sienkiewicz, and Lenore Watkins—
All that life offers—
joy, happiness, disappointments, tragedy, sadness,
experiences, successes, opportunities, and crossroads—
is especially wonderful and meaningful
when we have the good fortune
to be surrounded by
steadfast, nurturing friends
throughout life.
I thank you for sharing your lives with me.

To
Michael Barger—
Fond childhood memories
include a boy with a bubbly, mischievous temperament,
and a free-spirit that was impossible to reign in,
although many tried.
His love of life was infectious.
As a child, he made me laugh with his never-ending antics.
And, although he is no longer with us,
his leaving brought me the unexpected gift
of a renewed love for gardening,
as it offered me peace and comfort.
He shall continue to have a special place in my heart.
May his children always have loving
memories of their father.

Acknowledgments

I am deeply grateful to the people who have been directly responsible for bringing *The Visual Dance—Creating Spectacular Quilts* to fruition. It has been a wonderful experience working with the C&T Publishing family during the writing of this manuscript. I appreciate the encouragement and enthusiasm given by Tom, Carolie, Tony, and Todd Hensley.

Particular thanks goes to Louise Townsend, Diane Pedersen, and Todd Hensley who supported my decision to divide my original manuscript into two books, as it became evident there was too much information for one. Determining which concepts had to be withheld for a later publication was difficult. I appreciate the help they offered in this decision. It has been a joy having Louise Townsend as my editor. Her positive attitude, thoughtfulness, sensitivity, patience, as well as wise suggestions have made this experience a particularly pleasurable one for me.

I wish to thank the support staff whose many talents helped create this book. Kate Darnell is unsurpassed in creating hand-drawn illustrations, so I was thrilled that she was able to use her talents in *The Visual Dance*. It was wonderful having Joyce Lytle carefully attend to all of the technical details of this book. She was tireless in her efforts. I admire and appreciate Judith Moretz' superb ability as a copy editor. Her advice is always welcome, as I know her suggestions add strength to my writing. Also, it was lovely working with Bobbi Sloan, a seasoned graphic designer who added her wisdom and talents to make *The Visual Dance* visually outstanding. Thanks, also, to Judith Buskirk for her wonderful color exercises in Chapter Four. As in past books, I am extremely pleased that Ken Wagner was able to use his photographic talents on this project. His ability to photograph quilts beautifully adds visual impact to this book.

To all the contributing quiltmakers and textile artists, a special thanks is given. This book could never have been so visually successful without your lovely work. (A special case in point is the beautiful cover quilt made by Erika Odemer, a talented German textile artist.) It is wonderful to work with talented people who are willing to share their work with the rest of us. May you continue creating beautiful quilts.

I thank all of you for your talents, efforts, and generosity: Charlotte Andersen, Deirdre Amsden, Lois Arnold, Joy Baaklini, Ginny Baird, Ruth Bennett, Gail Biddle, Nancy Breland, Sharyn Craig, Sandi Cummings, Judy Dales, Sarah Dickson, Susan Duffield, Philomena Durcan, Joan Dyer, Anna Edwards, Cynthia England, Ann Fahy, Caryl Fallert, Flavin Glover, Barbara Friedman, Marie Fritz, Beth Gilbert, Alison Goss, Lesly-Claire Greenberg, Rosemarie Guttler, Jane Hall, Gloria Hansen, Lauralee Hanson, Irma Gail Hatcher, Laura Heine, Linda Hillan, Pat Hitchcock, Lois Horton, Vicki Hurst, Martie Huston, Yoshiko Ishikura, Jane Kakaley, Anita Krug, Sylvia Kundrats, Nobuko Kubota, Kari Lane, Jean Ray Laury, Mickey Lawler, Libby Lehman, Kay Lettau, Shawn Levy, Pat Magaret, Marion Marias, Judy Mathieson, Grania McElligott, Maureen McGee, Jay Moody, Narrows Connection Quilt Guild, Miriam Nathan-Roberts, Helen Newlands, Velda Newman, Sharon Norbutas, Regula Nussbaumer, Erika Odemer, Sonja Palmer, Karen Perinne, Caroline Perisho, Shirley Perryman, Donna Pringle, Kaye Rhodes, Janice Richards, Wendy Richardson, Mary Ann Rush, Ginny Sands, Junko Sawada, Linda Schmidt, Donna Schneider, Lorraine Simmons, Judy Sogn, Doreen Thompson, Daniele Todaro, Carol Ann Wadley, Donna Warnement, Judy White, Juanita Yeager, and Sylvia Zeveloff.

I also wish to thank conference sponsors, organization members, educational faculties, quilt guilds, and editors who have invited me to teach, lecture, write, and share my ideas and knowledge. As well, I am filled with gratitude for the individuals who have participated in these activities over the years. I am overwhelmed by your wonderful support, encouragement, and friendship. It is because of you, and for you, that this book has been written.

An Exciting Journey Into the World of Design

Dozens of books are written each year to help the quilt-maker increase and enhance her technical skill. Rarely, however, does anyone address the visual qualities of a quilt, even though this is an extremely important and necessary part of any artwork's success. Because of my own struggle to create lovely quilts, and because design and construction are so intricately interlocked in quiltmaking, I have chosen to write *The Visual Dance—Creating Spectacular Quilts*.

As a novice quiltmaker, it never occurred to me to be attentive to a quilt block's design potential or its overall visual beauty. Instead, I was totally engrossed with the technical application of constructing the quilt. As I gained more experience, I became aware that not all traditional designs produced lovely results. I noticed quilts made from the same traditional pattern could have wildly different visual results. For instance, a star-designed quilt could run the gamut of a show-stopper to a pleasing presentation to a mundane offering to even a visual disaster. I also realized my quilts' visual results were uneven—and often not what I really envisioned.

As my work developed, my quest for learning how to create beautiful quilts increased. I no longer wanted to spend time, money, and energy making quilts of dubious visual success. So I became interested in studying color. This exploration led me to a new realization—that color was only one part of a quilt's design. If I wanted to create a visually successful quilt, I also needed to concern myself with the other important components of design. This was a novel idea for me. With some natural hesitation, I began experimenting with the various aspects of design, so that I could strengthen this weak link in my artistic development.

My biggest stumbling block in this journey was my inability to translate design books' information into meaningful direction for my own work. Eventually I turned to nature for guidance, as it had given me such wonderful examples in my color study. I found examples of beautiful design practices exhibited in my natural surroundings. I share these findings with you in *The Visual Dance*.

In addition to presenting the design elements and principles, I have also addressed many design problems that occur frequently in quilts—with possible solutions. Quilts with particular design problems are discussed. Suggestions for increasing the visual beauty of quilts such as sampler, medallion, and round-robin designs are given. Fabric selection, border application, and innovative quilting suggestions are covered. Also offered are many traditional block patterns, including some I have created especially for you.

This book can easily be used as a companion resource with *The Magical Effects of Color*. I hope reading *The Visual Dance* will give you the incentive and foundation to investigate and explore further the fascinating subject of design. May it also give you the confidence to create captivating designs that reflect the unique and wonderful expression of your own sense of artistic beauty.

Read, enjoy, and create!

Joen

A lovely quilt that beckons us to pause and admire its beauty is not haphazardly planned. Instead, its magical effect is brought about through the blending of the maker's imagination and the elements and principles of design. Even the simplest pattern can captivate us with its graceful subtlety or dramatic flair. We are naturally drawn to beautiful designs and compelled to investigate them further. For the quilter who has developed her natural artistic inclination, this visually successful design process is clearly intuitive. For those of us who have shied away from artistic expression, the creative process must be thoughtfully planned.

Clearly there is no one right way to create a design that fascinates or satisfies everyone. There is, however, an established manner of working that increases the beauty and success of any design. These basics are founded in the practices of nature—our world's most influential and successful designer. You can realize a multitude of ideas and achieve great design success by both observing nature at work and using your observations as a personal guideline.

This book is not a treatise of design demands or strict rules. These guidelines are not meant to be rigidly followed, as doing so would destroy your personal power of creative intuition and individuality. To be inflexible with design's elements and principles is contrary to the true meaning of artistic expression. Therefore, *The Visual Dance—Creating Spectacular Quilts* is a presentation of nature's design basics to help you build a design foundation from which to develop your personal style. Included are a multitude of ideas for you to thoughtfully contemplate. I hope you will use these suggestions to blend your intuitive sense with sound design practices, and thereby create your own beautiful interpretive art.

I invite you to join me in a journey into the world of design. This is an excursion that focuses on beauty and creative expression. You will have the opportunity to indulge yourself in those areas that fit your own personal interests and needs. I embarked on a similar endeavor more than two decades ago and have never regretted the opportunities it has provided me. I welcome your company. . . .

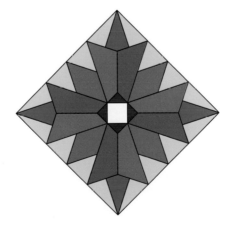

1. PIECE AND QUIET, 1993, 80" x 64"
Cynthia England, Houston Texas
This stunning quilt (shown on the facing page) is a departure from Cynthia's earlier traditional designs. With this new adventure, Cynthia is putting glimpses of her world into spellbinding quilts. Using photographs as her design foundation, Cynthia creates unbelievable impressionistic fabric reproductions. Both piecing and appliqué techniques are used. Photo: Ken Wagner.

Setting the Visual Stage

Excitement runs high when you contemplate beginning a new quilt. Your adrenaline flows, your mind races, and your fingers itch to get started. But wait—there are a few items yet to consider before your rotary cutter hits the cloth. Section One introduces you to a wealth of ideas, design basics, and other information to contemplate, prior to beginning construction. With these basics in mind, each quilt you make will be beautiful, exciting, and fun to create!

Welcome to the wonderful world of visual design....

Chapter One

The Emotional Power of Art

Our lifetime experiences, interactions, and teachings are the building blocks for our own unique creative personalities. Of prime importance to this creative spirit are the places we have called home within our lifetimes. Our hearts respond forcefully to these environmental influences; they reflect keenly within our creative souls. If we pause to think about the collective contrasts between all our lives, we have a better understanding of why each of us responds differently to individual quilts and other art. This understanding lessens our need to demand that our responses echo everyone else's, or even to expect that other people's preferences match our own.

Some have lived their lives in bustling cities filled with masses of humanity. Colorful neon lights beckon their attention, while tall, sleek skyscrapers reflect fascinating images on glass sides. The city's power is electrifying; its people thrive on fast-paced energetic activity. The city dazzles its residents with opportunities, cultural events, and diverse activities. Art created by these residents often exudes this excitement and the energy generated by the city. It is usually complex, detailed, and closely contained.

Others have lived in small, quiet, comfortable, slow-paced towns. Here, sturdy stone or brick buildings stand quietly in elegant grace, subtly reflecting the power of stability and slow change. The people here have proud traditions bound by generations of friendships and loyalties. Their art reflects their caring attitude and satisfaction with life. Often, it also closely mirrors the strength of their traditions and the power of their beliefs.

Rolling farmlands, with crops standing tall waiting for harvest, are home to many. Isolation is part of life here, since the closest neighbors may be miles away. Independence is a strong trait among those who live here. People must rely on their own hands and the land's bounty to live. Far in the distance, a thunder cloud may loom, and a flock of birds may appear, as silence prevails. Simplicity of life brings a peaceful contentment to those who love the land. Frequently, the art of this group reflects a feeling of wide open spaces through clean, strong lines. Deep feelings of solitude and respect for the land, poignantly emphasized, captivate the viewer.

Others are mesmerized by waves beating against a rocky shore. A foghorn calls in the distance as the cloud layer envelops the earth in a thick gray blanket. The smell of salt water is addictive to the soul, and it often seems as if no one else is present in this world. Eagles and hawks silently catch wind currents, while the water moves in its fierce rhythmic beat. Coastal artists often create emotive art, employing powerful strength in color and line that reflects nature's intensity.

We live in a world of contrasts, which evoke strong memories and feelings in each of us. The quilter (artist) from the country can't really feel the sounds of the city without experiencing them herself. Likewise, the inland city dweller has no experience of listening to the desolate sound of crashing waves as the wind howls across an isolated beach. It is difficult, also, for the city dweller or townsperson to understand the depth of feeling for the earth held by someone who lives close to the land. Its smell and touch are powerful and deeply ingrained in the country dweller's soul.

Your past and present environments make up a great part of your individual uniqueness. Once aroused, the feelings you hold for these experiences can be powerful tools for developing your design style. Because of the strength of these influences, it is always best to create what you feel in your soul, rather than to create what you think others expect from you.

RECOGNIZING YOUR ARTISTIC PREFERENCES

When you make a quilt, you use design and color to express yourself and tell your visual story. It is important, then, to know what captures your spirit, what makes you excited, and what you think is beautiful. If you haven't already done so, take time to clarify your design preferences by observing a wide variety of art.

At a quilt exhibit, you may be drawn to the subtle or exquisite beauty of traditional designs; you may be equally fascinated by the innovative traditional quilts vibrating with color and splendid illusions. Then too, you may be spellbound by the more contemporary works of a wide variety of quilt artists. Perhaps you yearn to capture the essence of *all* these different styles in the quilt world.

At a museum, perhaps the intense colors and strong lines in Georgia O'Keeffe's paintings will cause your heart to beat fast. Or it may be the finely detailed, luminous paintings of Pissarro that thrill you. Your wonder may be aroused by the musical fluidity of Dale Chihuly's glass art, or the cleverness of Escher, or the expressively rugged style of Rodin's sculpture. Silence may intensify as you stand in awe before a painting by Monet. Or perhaps your taste leans more toward Joan Miró, Jackson Pollack, Stuart Davis, or Ben Shahn.

After researching your artistic tastes, you should recognize whether you prefer busyness or complexity over clean lines and simplicity. You should also know if you respond more to highly contrasting colors and values than to subtle changes. Your preference for either soft, gentle lines or sharp edges and dramatic shapes will also be apparent.

No one piece of art or single style is right for everyone. Your preferences are extremely important, because they belong to you. It does not matter, then, if your taste differs from others. Most assuredly, it is of little consequence or importance if you find yourself alone in your likes. Recognizing what styles of art you want to create and surround yourself with is one of the most important gifts you can give yourself.

LEARNING TO SPEAK THE LANGUAGE OF ART

Art is one of the most beautiful interpretive languages found in our world. It is universally shared by all and owned by none. It can be simplistic or complex, depending on the desires of the creator. It can elicit almost any emotion or thought. Art transcends all boundaries.

All language, whether verbal or non-verbal, gives us a way to organize our thoughts or feelings, in order to communicate with others. For example, if there were no organization or formal structure in the English language, we would use words haphazardly, resulting in ambiguous meaning. Ambiguity can happen whenever any language is carelessly used. It is extremely important, then, to learn the non-verbal language of visual arts, so you can successfully communicate your ideas. *Design* is the non-verbal language used to convey ideas, emotions, and tales in any visual art form—including quilts.

Design—The Key to Knowing the Language

If we ignore the importance of design, we leave the visual success of our work to chance. Once the important design concepts are learned, however, the doors to an exciting world open before us. Design is an easy language to learn, as we are surrounded by a multitude of beautiful, flawless examples in both art and nature. The incentive is great for learning, too, since creating visually successful artwork is our reward for attaining new-found knowledge.

THE ELEMENTS OF DESIGN

If you carefully look at a quilt or any other work of art, you will see that each piece usually includes lines, shapes, direction, color, value, scale, proportion, and texture. These are referred to as the *elements of design*. Sometimes volume is included in this category of elements. You can create a multitude of designs and elicit many different moods by the way you arrange these elements.

THE PRINCIPLES OF DESIGN

As you arrange these elements, you intuitively strive to create unity through rhythm and harmony. Your inner sense also aspires to find visual balance and focus. Your eyes seek contrast to enhance interest. This intuitive need to arrange the elements into a visually pleasing artwork uses the *principles of design* to accomplish your goals.

THE ROLES OF THE ELEMENTS AND PRINCIPLES OF DESIGN

Don't be fooled into thinking these elements and principles are dry, uninteresting parts of a design. Instead, think of them as a family of intriguing personalities. Each one performs a unique role. And, it is your responsibility to determine which element plays the leading role, which one is cast in a supporting position, and which one has only a trivial part in each of your creative endeavors.

The roles of these design elements change with each quilt you create. In one design, the main character may be shapes, with color playing second-fiddle. At another time, color may take on the major role, while shapes are hardly noticed. You emphasize the elements that best tell your visual story. You limit the role of those elements, which are not important in your interpretation.

Take time to meet this entire family of interesting design characters. Explore their possible uses. Their personality traits and idiosyncrasies should help you decide what you choose to emphasize in a particular design. Naturally, you will find yourself favoring certain elements, wanting to give them the greatest roles in your designs. You will also favor certain principles, making them the primary conveyors of your message.

Without a doubt, some elements will become quite endearing to you, while others definitely will impose on your good nature. How you use these elements and principles will define your own artistic style or design sense. Exploring these various personalities should be an enjoyable, fun-filled journey, since it will enable you to create wonderful quilts (or other art) that reflect your personality and design sense.

Enjoy your journey!

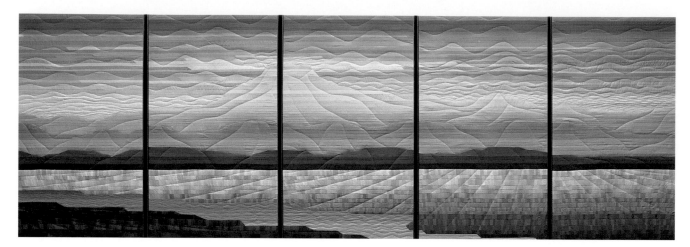

2. SPRINGTIME IN THE VALLEY, 1986, 14' x 4'6"
Joen Wolfrom, Fox Island, Washington
A five-piece work of art celebrating the birth of spring each year. The bulb fields of the Puyallup Valley are alive with color as the stately Mt. Rainier looms in the background. Photo: Ken Wagner, Seattle, Washington.

3. HOT AUGUST NIGHT, 1990, 60" x 75"
Joen Wolfrom, Fox Island, Washington
Sharply angled lines, continuously repeated, often create the effect of movement, excitement, or energy. Photo: Ken Wagner

4. Fractured Wedding Ring, 1991, 68" x 78"
Grania McElligott, Naas, Ireland
Closed curves evoke a feeling of completion.
The use of many fabrics adds interest to the
design. Photo: Tony Hurst, Ireland

5. Melodious Wave, 1984, 60" x 30"
Joen Wolfrom, Fox Island, Washington
Open curves create a free-flowing movement.
Toned hues are used for the dominant scale.
Quilting lines are used to enhance the design.
Photo: Ken Wagner

6. SAILS, 1992, 58" x 47"
Mickey Lawler,
West Hartford, Connecticut
Diagonal lines enhance the illusion of motion. In this quilt, based on a painting by Lyonel Feininger, one feels as if the sailboat is skipping through the water with ease. Most fabrics were hand-painted by Mickey. Photo: Jack McConnell, Connecticut

7. FAR AWAY FROM HOME, 1989, 44" x 40"
Mickey Lawler,
West Hartford, Connecticut
An adventure of mind and eye results when the lines of design are suggestive, as in this quilt, rather than clearly defined. It allows our imagination to participate in the design. Photo: Jack McConnell, Connecticut

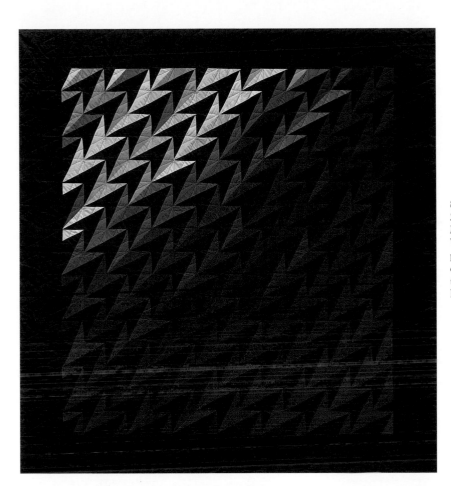

8. CUPID'S DART, 1986, 72" x 78"
*Sarah A. Dickson, San Antonio, Texas, and
Maureen H. McGee, Lansing, Kansas*
With the play of fabric and color, this traditional
pattern looks very contemporary. The gradation
of colors and strong diagonal line allows the eyes
to be led across the surface of the quilt. Photo:
Ken Wagner

9. PIÑATA, 1988, 56" x 68"
Jay Moody, Falls Church, Virginia
Sometimes a line will disappear intermittently throughout
a design, forcing the eyes to follow its suggestive path, as
in this quilt. This design was inspired by an antique Pennsylvania Dutch design. Hand-pieced and quilted. Photo:
Jinny Beyer

10. GALWAY HOOKERS, 1984, 72" x 72"
Ann Fahy, Galway, Ireland
This quilt is named after Galway's sailing boats. Triangles and
squares were used to create the boats. Some blocks were reversed
to give the appearance of reflections in the water. The blocks
placed in diagonal lines created another pattern. To get the narrow pointed sail, the rectangular triangle was cut in half. Photo:
Courtesy of the artist

11. CELTIC PEONY ROSE, 1990, 84" x 100"
Philomena Durcan, Sunnyvale, California
This beautifully balanced medallion quilt was created with Philomena's Celtic bias-appliqué technique (see Sources). Philomena has enhanced her design by setting the oval medallion in a rectangular format. Hand-appliquéd and quilted. Photo: Courtesy of the artist

12. CELTIC CLAN, 1991, 52" X 72"
Philomena Durcan, Sunnyvale, California
The vertical design of this quilt has been
strengthened by repeating the vertical lines in the
quilt's shape. Philomena's Celtic bias-appliqué
technique has been used to create this design.
Hand-appliquéd and quilted. Photo: Courtesy of
the artist

13. BLACKBIRDS OVER THE CORN, 1992, 78" X 84"
Marie Goyette Fritz, San Diego, California
The birds, seemingly coming from beyond the
quilt's surface, create a strong visual feeling of
motion with their diagonal path. Inspired by an
antique quilt, this quilt was constructed and quilted entirely by hand. Photo: Ken Wagner

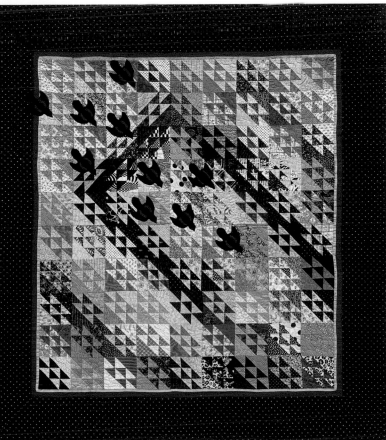

The Power of Line

THE LINE COMES ALIVE

The common line is so much a part of our lives, we rarely think about its importance or its many personality traits. Line allows us to print, write, doodle, sketch, and draw. Actually, line could be considered one of our most important inanimate companions. What else besides a line will move, stretch, contort, and curve itself simply to be, or do, whatever we wish?

A line is simply a group of continuous dots, which connect together. Although a line shows both length and width, length is usually its focus. Not only can a line be functional, helping us with our many tasks, it can be beautifully artistic and interpretive. Line can show elegance, nervousness, strength, softness, ambiguity, or harshness. For instance, calligraphy brings to line a most beautiful, elegant style of functional art. Illustrators, masters of line, can make simple lines into beautiful drawings that promote expressive ideas. Even cartoonists are great line manipulators. They can take a simple line and twist it this way and that to create forms that make us laugh. Notice the personality changes and visual impact of line in the illustrations and photos throughout this chapter.

Artists use their tools to draw lines that generate different emotional effects. A delicate line, a short pointillist stroke, a strong, wide brush stroke—all create different visual effects (Figure 2-1). Line can be asked to fulfill even broader tasks, such as defining edges, making contours, or creating a wide array of shapes (Figure 2-2). Line can even be used to convey the idea of movement (Figure 2-3).

Figure 2-2. Line can be used to define edges, make contours, and create a wide array of shapes.

Figure 2-1. A delicate line, a short pointillist stroke, a strong, wide brush stroke—all create different visual effects.

Figure 2-3. Line can be used to convey the idea of movement.

Figure 2-4. Vertical Line shows strength. Towering trees stand before us with strong visual strength. Photo by the author

Figure 2-5. Skyscrapers symbolize a vibrant, strong city. Photo by the author

THE PERSONALITY OF LINE

The Strength of Vertical Line

A towering tree stands before us with its evergreen boughs draped elegantly around its stately trunk (Figure 2-4). It is, indeed, the tree with the loftiest reputation, and generally the most revered in the land. Even though this tree may be no more important than any other inhabitant of the forest, we unconsciously grant it supreme honor in the environment. It has an image of strength, of power, even of authority. Clearly, the tall vertical line suggested by this tree is a symbol of strength.

Strength, calmness, motion, anxiety, and ideas can be emphasized by using one certain line style. It is fascinating to realize our eyes and mind can translate a simple line into such visual impact, even when it is only pencil thin.

In painting, photography, and quiltmaking, the design is not created merely through line. Often, the design line may be suggestive rather than actual. It can change simply by moving colors, values, and shapes throughout the design surface.

In traditional quiltmaking, geometric shapes and quilting lines enhance linear design. Often, there is interplay between the shape's movement and our perception of the line. Through this interplay, we make our own interpretations of where the line is going. When linear design becomes an adventure of eye and mind, rather than a clearly defined statement, the result is visually exciting. This type of playful linear design may be thought of as suggestive or interpretive line (Photos 3, 7, and 10).

Figure 2-6. A tall church steeple, towering above a town's skyline, can be a symbolic sign of power and strength. Photo by the author

Figure 2-7. The expansive horizontal line of sea, land, and sky brings us a feeling of calm well-being. Photo by Winslow Barger

Figure 2-8. This pastoral setting brings a feeling of tranquillity to the viewer with its horizontal lines. Photo by the author

Our eyes and minds confer power and strength on that which stands tall before us. Even the visual dominance of a city is seen in its lofty skyscrapers reaching far into the sky. Tall, vertical buildings have become the symbol for a city that is vibrant and strong (Figure 2-5). Church steeples forging their way high above a town also allude to a formidable ascendancy (Figure 2-6). Tall people are given special treatment and significance in our society. We often reward them with power and authority simply because of their vertical stature.

So it is that vertical line leads with silent sovereignty. If you wish to show power in your design, consider easing your job by using the strong, vertical line as the dominant direction of your design (Photo 12).

The Calmness of Horizontal Line

Subconsciously, we associate calmness and rest with horizontal lines. Perhaps that is because we sleep horizontally. The expansive horizontal line of sea and sky brings us a feeling of well-being (Figure 2-7). As we sail on water, the horizontal play of water and sky is mesmerizing. The same happens as we drive through vast farmlands. We become so overwhelmed with the peaceful line, we almost fall asleep. Looking across an expansive grassland, our stresses seem to disappear as the horizontal parkland brings us a feeling of solitude and tranquillity (Figure 2-8).

Thus, if you want to elicit a calming effect in your work, consider using a strong horizontal line as your major directional force. Naturally, to emphasize this tranquillity, colors, value changes, and other design elements must correspond in mood (see Photo 2).

Curved Line—Gentle Motion

A curve is a very soft, gentle line. It promotes a mellow mood (Figure 2-9). At the same time, a curve naturally suggests movement—lapping waves, floating bubbles, rolling balls, the aurora borealis. Even the curves of leaves and delicate flower petals beautifully blend the ideas of softness and direction or motion (Figure 2-10).

Open curves create a freer feeling. An ethereal effect may even be achieved with delicate curves (Photo 5). Closed curves that form circles add another dimension. There is a feeling of completion (Figure 2-11). Curiosity or wonder have been assuaged (Photo 4).

Figure 2-9. The soft, gentle curves of distant hills and mountains give us a feeling of serenity while moving our eyes across the landscape, while also suggesting movement and direction. Photo by the author

Figure 2-10. The curves of delicate flower petals bring serenity to the landscape, while gently promoting direction. Photo by the author

Figure 2-11. Circles give us a feeling of completion with their closed curves. The sun is one of nature's premier circular objects that we often use in our artwork. Photo by the author

A runner disappearing at the turn in the road, a raging mountain stream racing beyond our vantage point, and an ascending airplane heading into the clouds give us an even stronger impression of motion. These diagonal lines create a certain mystique or intrigue since we are not certain what goes on beyond our line of vision.

Diagonal lines, once begun, do not have to run to the quilt's edge. They can change directions, thereby enhancing movement and stimulating visual excitement. If the diagonal line moves in different directions within the design, motion is promoted very effectively within the design. If, on the other hand, the diagonal line continues to the edges of the quilt surface, our mind attempts to perceive what is happening beyond the quilt. If you want your quilt to suggest movement, consider using the diagonal line to help achieve this goal.

Diagonal Line—Enhancing Movement

A diagonal line enhances the illusion of motion (Figure 2-12). This illusion can be made subtle or strong, depending on how the design elements are used (Photos 6, 60, 66, and 78). At least three effects can be achieved through diagonal movement: a moving line that is halted in some way (see Photo 10); a moving line that moves beyond the visual surface, thereby intriguing us (Photos 8, 13, and 78); and a moving line that flows smoothly across the surface as it changes directions (Photos 68, 90, and 91). Even though each of these promotes the visual illusion of motion, each has its own individual appeal.

The diagonal configurations of stair steps, a slide, a flying kite, shooting stars, and a mountain slope all effectively encourage the feeling of continuation or possible motion. In these examples, there is a diagonal line with at least one ending point. This gives the impression of motion stopping or changing at some point.

Figure 2-12. A diagonal line enhances the feeling of movement. A diagonal sail promotes the feeling of motion. Photo by the author

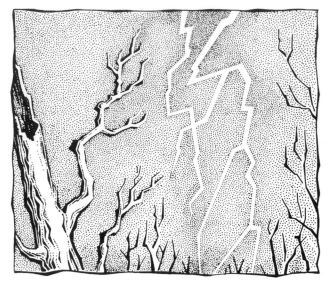

Figure 2-13. If diagonal lines are shortened, angled sharply, and continuously repeated, the effect is an angular or jagged line that can create excitement, energy, or anxiety.

Figure 2-14. Designs radiating from a center point naturally create balance, visual energy, and beauty. Photo by the author

Angular or Jagged Lines—Igniting Anxiety

If diagonal lines are shortened, angled sharply, and continuously repeated, the effect is an angular or jagged line. These lines can create excitement or energy (see Photo 3).

Angular or jagged lines can also play on our anxieties, often causing emotional discomfort. Some obvious jagged lines in nature help ignite our anxiousness. Lightning is an example of a natural phenomenon that promotes disquiet or anguish (Figure 2-13). Jagged, deep crevasses; gigantic, razor-sharp icicles hanging precariously from eaves; and the ragged teeth of a wolf all suggest danger.

You can strengthen the visual effect by changing the width of an angular line. A delicate line, jaggedly projected, can appear very sharp; a thick, jagged line may seem clunky or clumsy. It will not evoke the same feeling of danger, anxiety, or discomfort as the thinner line. If you want to startle or jar us with your design, consider using jagged or angular lines as your main design focus. Certainly, color and value choices must also play a great role in how strongly the anxiety is portrayed.

Lines Radiating from a Center Point

Lines radiating from a central point can be exciting and energizing (Figure 2-14). These designs often give the illusion of lines moving on forever (Photos 53 and 103). A radiating design can be placed anywhere within the surface area, as long as it is visually balanced. These lines can be straight, curved, angular, or any combination of these.

More Linear Traits

The actual presence of line is not always necessary. Sometimes a line will disappear intermittently throughout the design, creating an illusion of line that forces your eyes to follow its path. Then, it becomes a mere suggestion of line. This suggestive line can add intrigue to your design (Photos 9, 10, and 30).

You may incorporate more than one type of line in your design. This can be done successfully as long as the lines do not compete against each other. One linear direction must remain dominant, while any other directional lines join to enhance or act as an accent (Figure 2-15).

Figure 2-15. Incorporating more than one kind of line in a design can create a compelling design. One linear direction must retain its visual power over the other. Here, the diagonal line of the rail fence creates a stronger force than the quiet horizontal line in the background. Photo by the author

THE FLOW OF DIRECTION

Most art, including quilts, is created in a square, vertically rectangular, or horizontally rectangular format. The quilt's purpose and its design direction should dictate this shape. Almost always, one shape will be a better choice than another. If you create a strongly vertical design, it is usually best to make your quilt a vertical rectangle (see Figure 2-16 and Photo 12).

If you take a strongly vertical design and place it in a horizontal configuration, the design impact is almost always lessened. It appears as though something is missing from the design. Your mind notes this confusion, and this competition results in visual distraction (Figure 2-17).

There are exceptions to the rule. If you have a strongly vertical design (tall trees), you could ignore this strong trait by emphasizing a close-up view of the trees. In doing so, you can change the focus by only showing a portion of the trees. If you place this in an exaggerated horizontal format, it can add an intriguing contrast rather than a conflict (Figure 2-19).

The least successful format for a rectangular design is a square, because it does not allow the design to move in its vertical direction. Thus, this particular shape often compromises the success of the vertical design (Figure 2-18).

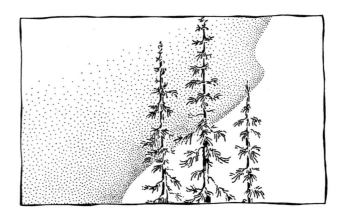

Figure 2-17. Confusing the flow of direction happens when a vertical design is placed in a horizontal format. The design's strength is diminished.

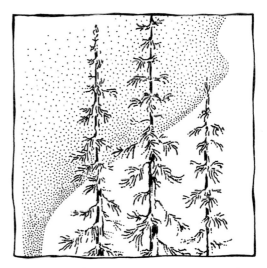

Figure 2-18. A design cannot accentuate its vertical strength when it is placed within a square, because there is not enough vertical space to create the flow of direction.

Figure 2-16. Tall vertical lines suggested by these trees are a symbol of strength. By repeating the vertical direction through the overall shape of the picture, a design's vertical flow can reach its full potential.

Figure 2-19. Sometimes, the obvious directional flow of a design is ignored to accentuate another part of the design. In this illustration, the trees are merely used to enhance the horizontal view in the distance. If you accentuate another part of the design, use the format that best helps you achieve your purpose.

Figure 2-20. Calmness and rest are suggested through horizontal line. A strongly horizontal design is best placed in a horizontal format.

Figure 2-22. A strongly horizontal design placed in a square format is usually quite ineffective because the design is not allowed to flow.

If your design is clearly horizontal in nature, your quilt's shape should reiterate this quality (Photo 2). Attempt to repeat the design's direction through its shape whenever possible. By repeating the design's horizontal line, you accentuate the restful mood of the quilt (Figure 2-20). This is more a matter of choice with a wall quilt, but rather a moot point for a bed quilt.

Notice that when you make a strongly horizontal design into a vertical format, it subtly changes the effect. Forcing the design into a vertical shape confines its expansiveness. This results in a subtle loss of overall tranquillity. It can also unintentionally change the focus of the design (Figure 2-21).

Placing a horizontal design in a square format is usually visually unsuccessful because a square limits direction; the design is cut off before it has a chance to create direction. The results are disappointing (Figure 2-22).

Figure 2-21. A strongly horizontal design placed in a vertical format loses its calming mood. Also, by placing a horizontal design in a vertical format, the flow of the design is lessened. The beauty of the design is compromised.

The Square Quilt

With few exceptions, a square-shaped quilt is the most difficult with which to create a successful design. A square doesn't allow enough room for most designs to evolve, so the design's direction is most often compromised or lost. It is a good rule of thumb to stay clear of the square format unless it clearly enhances your design.

Designs that should be presented in a square format are those that radiate from the center (Figure 2-23; Photos 50, 53, and 56). The Log Cabin Barn Raising (Photo 70) is appropriate for a square quilt, because it builds its pattern concentrically from the center. Designs radiating from the center can look ill-conceived or unbalanced when they are put in a rectangular format (Figure 2-24).

A medallion quilt should repeat the shape of its central design. Therefore, a medallion quilt with a square or circular center is best presented as a square quilt (Photo 88), whereas an oval or vertically-centered medallion quilt looks better in a vertical shape (Photos 11 and 59).

Figure 2-23. Lines radiating from a design's center point can create visual energy and excitement. A radial design is almost always best placed in a square format.

SQUARE QUILTS AS EXHIBIT REQUIREMENTS

Many national and regional quilt competitions and exhibits require entries be made in a square format, often even mandating the specific size. Those who make this arbitrary requirement probably are not aware that their decision compromises and restricts the creative flow of most designs.

If you find yourself faced with a size or shape requirement for an exhibition quilt, determine what kind of design you wish to create before committing to this assignment. If your design will be compromised by the size or shape requirement, consider how important the exhibit is to you. In the end, don't let other people's restrictions override your own creative potential.

Figure 2-24. A radial design placed in a rectangular format usually lacks success because there is visual imbalance.

ACTIVITIES AND EXTENDED LEARNING:

1. From calendars, books, and magazines, choose three pictures that show one of the following: (a) a strongly vertical design; (b) a strongly horizontal design; and (c) a design that radiates from the center. (These should not be pictures of quilts.) Make three copies of each chosen picture (black/white or color copies). Redesign each picture by cutting the picture into a vertical rectangle, a horizontal rectangle, and a square.

With each picture, select the view that works best. Choose the least effective one. Analyze the reasons why you made your decisions. Remember, the same considerations should be used when planning your quilts.

2. Look at quilts in quilt magazines and books. Notice the design directions in different quilts (vertical, horizontal, curved, diagonal, angular, or radiating from the center). After observing several quilts, which kind of line do you prefer? While examining these quilts, notice whether the shapes of the quilts agree with their design directions. How do you feel when they complement each other? How do you feel when they are in disagreement?

3. Select a block pattern that appears to give the impression of linear design. Make 15 to 20 copies of this block pattern (*i.e.*, 2" block size). After you have cut the blocks out, arrange them in a vertically shaped paper quilt. Then rearrange them into a horizontal design. Finally, make the blocks into a square shape. Which configuration did you like best for your design? Which one did you like the least? Repeat this same exercise with some of your favorite quilt blocks. Take the time to do this exercise prior to beginning any traditional block quilt.

4. Collect pictures of natural objects that use radial design for their linear direction. Study these objects; analyze what you like best in these designs. List your favorite features. Create your own design on paper, using these features for inspiration. Choose the technique(s) best suited for your design when planning your quilt.

5. Be aware of the pattern direction you like best. Attempt to use this new awareness in your future quilt design plans.

14. SPRING IN THE VALLEY, 1994, 37" x 44"
Marion Marias, Fresno, California
Using two-inch squares on-point, Marion created the impression of spring when the profusion of blossoms follow each other in rapid succession. The flower fields stretch to the green foothills below the towering snowcapped Sierras. Photo: Ken Wagner

15. WHEN EAST MEETS WEST, 1991, 68" x 60"
Pat Magaret, Pullman, Washington
This One Thousand Pyramids pattern was created with equilateral triangles. The border enhances the design, as it plays a secondary role through its related coloring. Photo: Courtesy of the artist

16. COME FLY WITH ME, 1992, 62" x 48"
Linda S. Schmidt, Dublin, California
This realistic quilt incorporated hand-painted fabrics for the sky and transparent lamé for reflections. To increase realism, Linda created three-dimensional waves. Photo: Ken Wagner

17. GARDEN LIGHT, 1990, 38" x 38"
Sandi Cummings, Moraga, California
Garden Light incorporates multi-colored, diagonally placed rectangular strips to create its design. Machine-quilted by Sandy Klop. Photo: Courtesy of the artist

18. CHALLENGE WITH RED, 1994, 146CM X 150CM
Regula Nussbaumer, St. Gallen, Switzerland
Drama has been created using on-point squares. The strength of the red vertical lines is accentuated by the black-and-white background fabrics. Photo: Courtesy of the artist

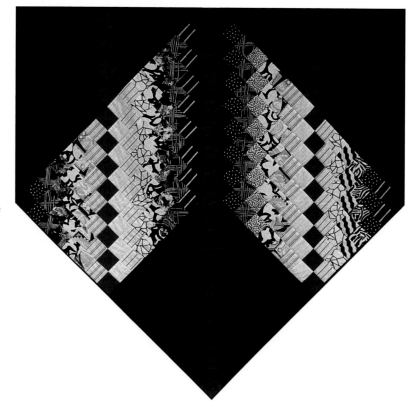

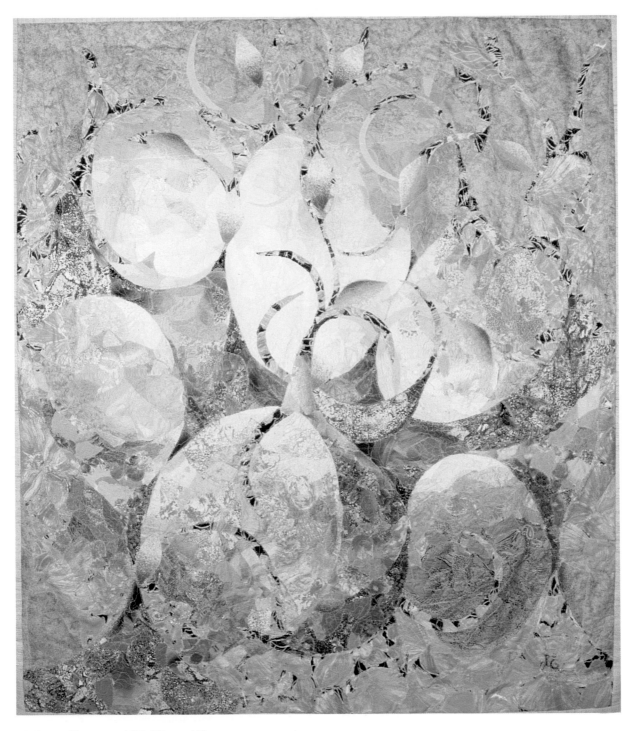

19. ROUDO VEUEZIANO, 1992, 150CM X 135CM
Rosemarie Guttler, Kuppenheim, Germany
Organic shapes can make beautiful, flowing designs, as in *Roudo Veueziano*. This quilt
art is quite tranquil because the flowing curves are partnered with soft, subtle colors.
Photo: Courtesy of the artist

20. THE HILLS ARE ALIVE
1991, 78" x 62"
Pat Magaret, Pullman, Washington
Pat has ingeniously used triangles
to create the trees and mountains
in this delightful picture quilt. The
sky is made from nine-patch
squares. Photo: Pat Magaret

21. BLUE ROSE, 1992, 63" x 80"
Sharon Norbutas, Camarillo, California
This Ocean Waves quilt is an example of color
family, scale and value working together to create
fascinating design play in a traditional design.
Nine friends each contributed four blocks in blue
and rose hues. Color interpretation varied greatly;
this allowed the design to become more effective,
as the colors vibrated against each other. Photo:
Ken Wagner

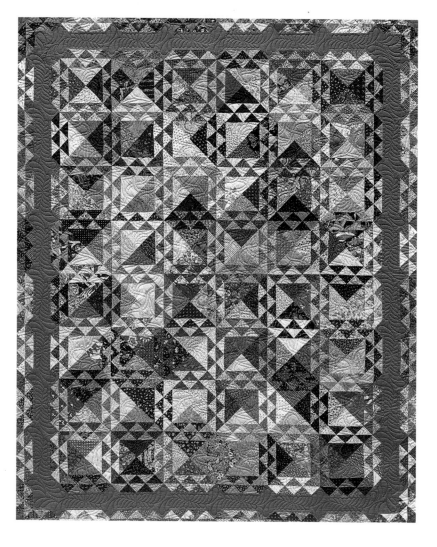

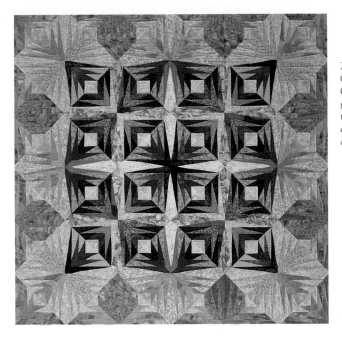

22. AWAKENINGS, 1992, 66" x 66"
Gloria Hansen, Hightstown, New Jersey
Gloria's original design is based on a repeat block she drew on graph paper. This pattern uses obtuse triangles. Gloria arranged the design so that the concentration of color occurred in the center, and then extended outward. Machine-pieced; hand-quilted. Photo: Courtesy of the artist

23. OPALS IN THE WEB, 1992, 29" x 29"
Pat Magaret, Pullman, Washington
This beautiful Spider Web quilt is created with isosceles triangles. The opalescent color effect is due to the subtle differences in the hues and color scales used in the triangular pieces. Photo: Ken Wagner

24. LIFTING FOG, 1992, 36" x 36"
Pat Magaret, Pullman, Washington
Small squares have been used to create this design of value contrasts. A wide variety of prints are used effectively. Hues are toned to create the illusion of fog. Pat is the co-author of *Watercolor Quilts* (see Sources). Photo: Ken Wagner

25. GARDEN PARTY, 1989, 49" X 61"
Caryl Bryer Fallert, Oswego, Illinois
This quilt illustrates how powerfully the design elements of line, shape, direction, color, and value can work together to create a spectacular work of art. The design for this quilt was based on a series of thumbnail sketches and color renderings. The sketches began with organic shapes derived from nature. The design was developed by repeating these shapes at various angles. Photo: Courtesy of the artist.

26. WANDERLUST II, 1992, 41" X 46"
Libby Lehman, Houston, Texas
Piecing and intricate stitching give this exquisite quilt dimension and vibrancy. The rich, dark background makes a wonderful backdrop for the exciting color changes used in this non-objective design. Photo: Courtesy of the artist

27. TRIP AROUND THE WORLD: BON VOYAGE, 1991, 70" X 84"
Libby Lehman, Houston, Texas
This quilt combines a variety of techniques to create excitement and interest. This is an excellent example of non-objective art. Photo: Courtesy of the artist

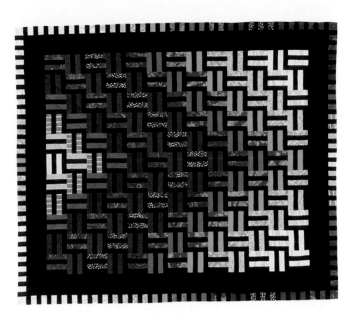

28. GRADATION, 1989, 162CM X 142CM
Regula Nussbaumer, St. Gallen, Switzerland
A rectangular shape is used for the traditional pattern Rail Fence. In this quilt, Regula has used rectangular shapes to create wonderful color movement in an analogous color scheme. Photo: Courtesy of the artist

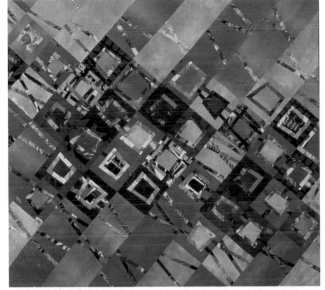

29. FAMILY TIES I, 1992, 40" X 44"
Sandi Cummings, Moraga, California
A beautiful work of art using non-objective shapes, Sandi has created an artwork with wonderful design applications. Machine-quilted by Sandy Klop. Photo: Courtesy of the artist

30. JOURNEY HOME, 1988, 30" X 66"
Janice Ohlson Richards, Vaughn, Washington
An abstract design of salmon returning home to their spawning grounds was created through fracturing the block pattern. A wide variety of fabrics was used to enhance the imagery. Photo: Ken Wagner

The Fascination of Shapes

Shapes are the workhorses of design. Their forms enable us to create anything our minds imagine. Since shapes play such an important role in our designs, we are wise to familiarize ourselves with these tools of our trade.

Our world is crowded with shapes of many different sorts. Most shapes fall into five categories, or families: natural, organic, abstract, non-objective, and geometric. Each family of shapes has its own visual appeal, as well as its own strengths and weaknesses. Each has the ability to convey certain moods. Members within each family also help transmit moods and further accentuate design goals.

Geometric shapes are the most prevalent in traditional piecing. Geometric and natural shapes are used in most appliqué. Many contemporary quilters enjoy the freedom of expression possible with organic, abstract, and non-objective forms. Our design style and personal flair determine the family of shapes we use in each quilt we make.

NATURAL SHAPES

We live with natural shapes in our daily lives. A daffodil blowing in the breeze, birch leaves weeping over a dry creek bed, the strong linear grooves in the bark of an old fir tree, the sand dunes of the desert, the silhouette of a hoot owl perched on telephone wires, a cat slinking into the meadow—these are a hint of the multitude of shapes in nature. Trees, flowers, bushes, valleys, rolling hills, and mountains are only a few forms in the family of natural shapes. Whether in shadow or brilliant sun, these images are distinct and easily recognizable (Figure 3-1).

In the past, appliqué was traditionally created in folk art style. It was not unusual to use triangles for trees or mountains. Bushes became circles. Prior to the late 1980s, most scenic quilts were done in this style. Pat Magaret's *The Hills Are Alive* (Photo 20) is related to this folk art style with its ingenious triangular trees and mountains. Currently, we are seeing a new genre of landscape quilts being created—one that portrays the world quite realistically (Photo 1 on page 9; Photos 16, 69, 85, 86, and 87).

Figure 3-1.
Natural shapes, such as a flower or leaves, are immediately recognizable to us. They are a part of our everyday life. Photo by the author

ORGANIC SHAPES

Organic shapes have free-flowing lines. They appear to be loose, non-specific, non-rigid shapes. Neither traditions nor rules encumber them. Organic and natural shapes often share a close kinship, sometimes overlapping. For instance, large, gentle, puffy clouds can be considered both natural and organic. Honey running across a plate can form wonderful organic shapes. Spilt milk also creates beautiful shapes worthy of duplicating. Puddles, grease stains, and indistinct shadows—all have the organic characteristics of an amorphous mass (Figure 3-2).

Sometimes nature outdoes herself in forming organic shapes. Free-flowing, undulating curtains of colorful light in the aurora borealis are breathtaking. The form is almost ethereal in its movement. The beautiful flow of lava slowly creeping down a mountainside is also awe-inspiring. These fluid forms, even though they are not technically living parts of nature's scheme, are organic in shape. Organic shapes make beautiful, flowing designs, whether in paint or fabric. They can be tranquil if the flowing curves are used with gentle color choices (Photos 19 and 75). In contrast, a curve's delicate softness can be transformed into a dynamic design with strong, vibrant colors (Photo 25).

Figure 3-2. Shadows may be part of the division of organic shapes with their free-flowing lines. Organic shapes appear loose, non-specific, and non-rigid. Photo by the author

ABSTRACT SHAPES

Quilters sometimes use abstract shapes in their designs. These shapes may use a combination of natural, organic, or geometric shapes; abstract shapes often borrow from other families to give us design clues. Shapes can be skewed, stretched, compacted, or combined to tease the mind by making a visual suggestion (Figure 3-3). For example, an abstract fish may not look realistic, but a successfully created abstract design gives us enough clues to allow our minds to guess correctly at the intended imagery. Many quiltmakers enjoy working in this less restricted style.

Now, in the mid-1990s, we see a growing number of quilts created in the abstract style. Abstract shapes are often made from a wide variety of geometric (or geometric-like) shapes. It is fun to create abstractly, because the style is so non-restrictive and creatively unpredictable. Working in this style allows improvisation. The completed quilt is often different from the original plan, because the quilter allows intuition to take over.

Figure 3-3. Shapes can be skewed, stretched, or compacted to give an abstract visual impression. With the wind blowing, these trees are no longer clearly defined. They have an abstract appearance. Photo by the author

Additional interest and impact are created through color and fabric manipulation. Two abstractly created quilts are *Galway Hookers* (Photo 10) and *Journey Home* (Photo 30). The subject matter of each relates to the sea (fishing boats and salmon). Each artist has achieved her imagery differently. It's exciting to see how two minds tackle related designs.

NON-OBJECTIVE SHAPES

Non-objective shapes are related to the abstract family; however, they do not represent any idea or object (Figure 3-4). This style is noted for its ability to be both non-representational and improvisational. Non-objective forms fit into no other category, although they may borrow from all the other groups. Certainly, many non-objective styled quilts have a geometric kinship (Photo 17).

Non-objective shapes are not required to have the discipline of a geometric shape. They are bound by no rules. If the quilter wants to put a bubble on the perimeter of a square, she may. Then, of course, the shape is no longer a square. In essence, whatever the creator imagines or wishes to do on the design surface may be done. Three beautiful examples of non-objective art are *Family Ties I* (Photo 29), *Trip Around the World: Bon Voyage* (Photo 27), and *Wanderlust II* (Photo 26). The latter quilt has been further enhanced by intricate stitching to give more dimension.

Figure 3-4. Non-objective shapes do not represent any idea or object, nor do they have to meet any requirements. This detailed view of Madrona (Arbutus) tree bark is an example of non-objective shapes. Photo by the author

Geometric Shapes

The division of geometric shapes is the major family used in traditional piecing. These shapes are enormously collaborative, often subtly surfacing within the other categories. This family of shapes is large and diverse. Some family members always look the same (*e.g.*, squares), while others have a wide array of personalities (*e.g.*, triangles). Because we spend a great deal of time using geometric shapes, we need to look more closely at these design tools. To help refresh our memories and provide a working foundation, a variety of geometric shapes is discussed here. This information helps us draft patterns with ease. Characteristics, strengths, weaknesses, and other observations are included.

The Rectangle

By definition, a rectangle is any four-sided shape with four 90° angles at the corners (Figure 3-5). Thus, a square is a type of rectangle. However, in the context of quilt-making, we refer to rectangles as four-sided, 90°-angled shapes with two short sides and two long sides.

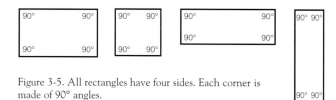

Figure 3-5. All rectangles have four sides. Each corner is made of 90° angles.

Rectangles come in a wide range of appearances. The long sides of a rectangle may be only slightly longer than the short sides, making the shape appear like an inaccurately drawn square. Or the two long sides may be greatly stretched, allowing us to perceive a sense of direction.

The rectangle has great capacity for change, allowing for wonderful effects. It is one of the most useful geometric shapes. In both traditional and contemporary quilt-making, we see many uses for rectangular shapes. Rail Fence is a simple traditional rectangular pattern (Figure 3-6). It has never been prettier than in *Gradation* (Photo 28). In *Southwest Hidden Wells* (Photo 132), thin, bright rectangular shapes create square boundaries.

A horizontally placed rectangle gives a calming, restful effect. A strongly vertical rectangle promotes strength and upward direction. If a rectangle is placed diagonally in the design, it can create linear movement. *Garden Light* (Photo 17) uses rectangular strips to create its design.

Figure 3-6. Rectangular shapes are often used in block patterns. Rail Fence, a traditional block pattern, uses narrow rectangular shapes.

The Stable Square

A square is a specific type of rectangle: it has four equal sides. Naturally, all corners are 90° angles. This is the most stable of all shapes, always predictable, never varying except in size.

Squares are uninventive and unimaginative. The square's purpose, therefore, is to play a supporting role in the company of other shapes or elements. It is a great filler in a design. When the square is the only shape in the design, monotony can prevail. To keep this from happening, we need to elevate another element in the design to major importance and downplay the shape. This can be done quite successfully through color or value changes. Quilts illustrating the diversity of designs created with squares include Photos 14, 18, and 24. Common designs using only squares are Nine Patch Chain (Figure 3-7) and Trip Around the World (Figure 3-8; Photos 93 and 94).

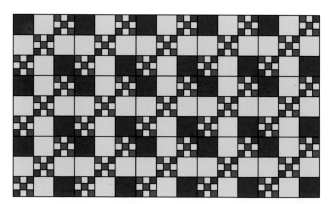

Figure 3-7. Many designs use squares to create their design. One example is the Nine Patch Chain.

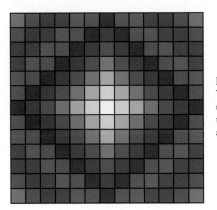

Figure 3-8. Trip Around the World uses a concentric pattern of squares to create its design.

The Multi-Faceted Triangle

A triangle has three sides and three angles that equal 180°. Beyond that, triangles are a varied lot. Even though they are related by virtue of their three-sidedness, this family has diverse membership. The length and width of the sides and angles are the keys to any triangle's makeup. To use triangular shapes to their best advantage, be aware of their differences.

THE ISOSCELES TRIANGLE GROUP

The isosceles triangle is one of the most popular in quilt block designs. It is a triangle that has at least two identical sides and angles (Figure 3-9). These identical sides are considered legs of the triangle. The third side is considered the base.

Figure 3-9. Isosceles triangles have at least two identical sides and angles.

The traditional pattern Ocean Waves is an excellent example of a design using isosceles triangles (Figure 3-10; Photos 21 and 128). Another popular design incorporating isosceles triangles is Thousand Pyramids. Color and value changes are of prime importance in this design. An exquisite Thousand Pyramids quilt is Susan Duffield's *Mountain Sunrise* (Photo 74).

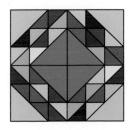

Figure 3-10. Ocean Waves is a pattern that uses isosceles triangles to create its fascinating design.

The longer the legs of the isosceles triangle's sides, the more pronounced the top is. The result is often a jagged look. In fact, a dogtooth effect can easily be created with thin, elongated isosceles triangles (Figures 3-11 and 3-12). It's hard to achieve a jagged effect with other kinds of triangles. The Spider Web pattern (Photo 23) is an example of a design using a multitude of isoceles triangles. Some shapes in the Mariner's Compass are also elongated isosceles triangles (Figure 3-13).

Figure 3-11. Tall isosceles triangles can create a jagged effect.

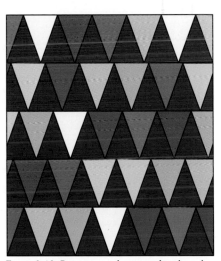

Figure 3-12. Patterns can be created with multiple jagged "dogtooth" isosceles triangles. Designs depend on colors, values, and textures used in the triangles.

Figure 3-13. Isosceles triangles are used in many circular patterns. The most pronounced triangles in this Mariner's Compass are isosceles triangles.

The Half-Square Triangle:
The 45-45-90 Right Triangle

One of the most frequently used isosceles triangles is formally called a 45-45-90 right triangle. It has two identical sides and two identical 45° angles. The third remaining angle is a right angle (90°). When you combine two identical 45-45-90 right triangles, they form a square. Thus, in the quilt world we identify these particular isosceles triangles as *half-square triangles* (Figure 3-14).

Figure 3-14. Half-square triangles are formed when a square is divided diagonally in half. These two identical triangles are isosceles.

Conversely, the opposite is true. If you divide a square diagonally in half, two half-square triangles are created. Hundreds of block designs use these half-square triangles to create their designs. They include Dutchman's Puzzle (Figure 3-15) and Square and a Half (Figure 3-17). These are probably the most stable looking of all the triangles.

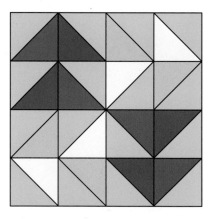

Figure 3-15. Dutchman's Puzzle is one of the many patterns that uses half-square triangles.

Squares can be divided even further by adding a second diagonal line between opposite corners. Four small triangles are created (Figure 3-16). These are still isosceles triangles, because they have two equal sides and two equal angles (45-45-90). In quilting, because four of these triangles can be put together to form a square, we call them *quarter-square triangles*. Many quilt designs cut squares into four triangles. An example of a design using quarter-square triangles is Square and a Half (Figure 3-17).

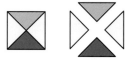

Figure 3-16. The four triangles created when a square is divided diagonally from all corners are called quarter-square triangles.

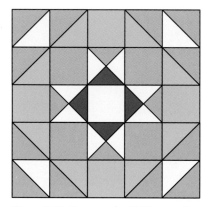

Figure 3-17. Square and a Half is one of many designs that uses both half-square triangles and quarter-square triangles.

Equilateral Triangles

An equilateral triangle is also an isosceles triangle. Its name describes its universal features: It has three equal sides and each angle contains 60° (Figure 3-18). Designs using only equilateral triangles are similar to those using only squares. They can be monotonous if no variety is added. Therefore, make certain another design element creates the major focus. Color play and value changes can develop into wonderful designs using these triangles. One such charming quilt created with equilateral triangles is Pat Magaret's *When East Meets West* (Photo 15).

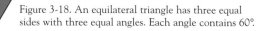

Figure 3-18. An equilateral triangle has three equal sides with three equal angles. Each angle contains 60°.

THE SCALENE TRIANGLE: THE TRIANGLE OF INEQUALITY

Scalene triangles have no equal sides or angles. The most popular scalene triangle used in quilting is the *30-60-90 right triangle* (Figure 3-19).

Figure 3-19. Scalene triangles have no equal sides or angles. The most common scalene triangle is the 30-60-90 right triangle.

When two 30-60-90 right triangles are placed together, they form a rectangle (Figure 3-20). Thus, in the quilt world we may call them *half-rectangle triangles*. Patterns using scalene triangles include Pin Wheel Square (Figure 3-21).

Figure 3-20. When two 30-60-90 right triangles are placed together, they form a rectangle. These are half-rectangle triangles.

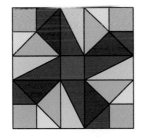

Figure 3-21. Patterns using scalene triangles that have been formed from rectangles include Pin Wheel Square.

ACUTE TRIANGLE

An acute object is one with a sharp point or tip. It stands to reason, then, that triangles with sharply pointed angles are called *acute triangles*. In order to be an acute triangle, all three angles of a triangle must be *less* than 90°. These triangles can have very prickly personalities. So, if you want to create images of porcupines, rugged mountains, or narrow pine trees in your geometric design, you may best do it by using acute triangles (Figure 3-22).

Figure 3-22. Acute triangles always have angles less than 90°. They can be used to create prickly imagery.

The most commonly used acute triangle in quiltmaking is the equilateral triangle (Figure 3-18 and Photo 15). All three of its angles are 60°. This triangle is also a member of the isosceles group because it has at least two equal sides. Common bonds such as these often allow shapes to overlap into different groups.

OBTUSE TRIANGLE

We refer to something as obtuse when it is blunt. An *obtuse triangle* spreads its sides out, making it flatter looking than other triangles. An obtuse triangle has one angle greater than 90° (Figure 3-23). Alone, it often looks awkward. However, an obtuse triangle is almost never seen without its mirror-image twin. When paired, obtuse triangles become beautiful shapes (Figure 3-24).

Figure 3-23. An obtuse triangle has one angle that is more than 90°. It has a spreading, flatter look than other triangles.

Figure 3-24. Two obtuse triangles placed together can create interesting designs with their mirror images.

Two sets of triangles are made when a rectangle is divided diagonally from all corners (Figure 3-25). One set is acute while the other is obtuse. All are isosceles.

Figure 3-25. When a rectangle is divided into fourths diagonally, two triangles will be tall and thin (acute), and two will be short and broad (obtuse). All are also isosceles.

Several sets of obtuse triangles can combine to create really beautiful designs. Traditional designs using obtuse triangles include Wedding Ring Glow (Figure 3-26), Cutting Edge (Figure 3-41), and Icelandic Poppy (Figure 3-42). Obtuse triangles are also either isosceles or scalene.

An obtuse triangle can become a diamond when it is paired with its opposite (Figure 3-24). Thus, diamonds split lengthwise become two obtuse triangles. Gloria Hansen has created a wonderful original design with obtuse triangles (Photo 22).

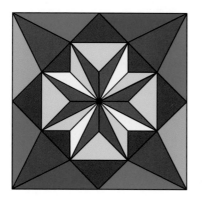

Figure 3-26. Obtuse triangles are used to create the inner design of Wedding Ring Glow (©1994 Joen Wolfrom).

Hexagon

A hexagon is a six-sided shape (Figure 3-27). We cherish several historic hexagon patterns such as Grandmother's Flower Garden. Besides the obvious hexagon patterns, other designs can be drawn with a six-sided shape. The Six-Pointed Star is an example (Figure 3-28 and Photo 109). A popular pattern created by using hexagon shapes is Tumbling Blocks (Figure 3-29). One beautiful example of this pattern is *Winchester Charm* (Photo 77).

Figure 3-27. A hexagon is a six-sided shape.

Figure 3-28. A Six-Pointed Star is made from a hexagon shape.

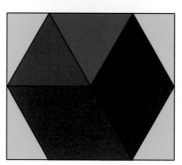

Figure 3-29. The Tumbling Block design is created from a hexagon.

Octagon

An octagon is an eight-sided shape (Figure 3-30). There is great potential to create interesting octagonal designs, although few traditional patterns include them. As in working with hexagons, one octagonal form is connected to another. The design can be quite intricate, since it can be broken into small sections. Octagonal designs include Puzzling Star (Figure 3-31) and Spider Web (Photo 23).

Figure 3-30. An octagon is an eight-sided shape.

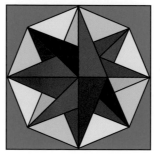

Figure 3-31. Interesting designs can be created with the octagonal shape. One example is Puzzling Star (©1994 Joen Wolfrom).

Trapezoid

A trapezoid is a four-sided shape with two parallel sides and two non-parallel sides. The parallel sides are referred to as the bases of the trapezoid (Figure 3-32). Although trapezoids rarely are used in historic traditional blocks, they can create beautiful interlocking designs.

Patterns using trapezoids include Rolling Square, Crowned Cross Variation, and Reflecting Ducks (Figures 3-33, 3-34, and 3-35). Other patterns that incorporate trapezoids in their designs are Through the Looking Glass and Hidden Star (both in the "Exciting New Designs" section on page 135).

Figure 3-32. A trapezoid is a four-sided shape with two parallel sides and two non-parallel sides.

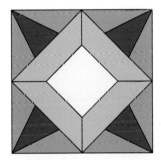

Figure 3-33. Trapezoids create interesting framing within a pattern. Rolling Square uses four trapezoids in its design (©1994 Joen Wolfrom).

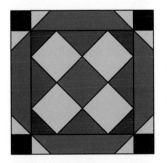

Figure 3-34. Trapezoids are used as borders to surround an inner design in some patterns such as Crowned Cross Variation.

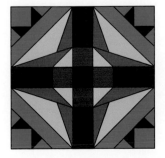

Figure 3-35. Reflecting Ducks, a variation of Duck Paddle, uses trapezoids in its design (©1994 Joen Wolfrom).

Diamonds

Diamonds are loved by a great many quilters because they help to make wonderful designs. To clarify, a diamond is a shape with four equal sides, which form two obtuse angles and two acute angles (Figure 3-36). Formally, diamonds are lozenges (a term we only use in math class). On close scrutiny, however, the quilt world uses the term "diamond" for other geometric shapes. Most quilt pattern diamonds are either kites (shapes with pairs of adjacent equal sides and no sides parallel; Figures 3-37 and 3-42) or parallelograms (four-sided figures with opposite sides parallel; Figures 3-38 and 3-40).

Figure 3-36. Formally, a diamond is a skewed square with four equal sides, which form two obtuse angles and two acute angles.

Figure 3-37. In quiltmaking, kites (a little-used geometric term) are considered diamond-shaped. Kite shapes have two sets of adjacent sides that are equal in length; no sides are parallel.

Parallelogram diamonds take on different personalities as a result of the angles used. In quilting, these diamonds are named for their angle. A 45° diamond is shaped by 45° angles (Figure 3-38). Godey's Design is a simple pattern using eight 45° diamonds (Figure 3-39). A 30° diamond is made from 30° angles (Figure 3-40). Cutting Edge uses 30° diamonds for its main focus (Figure 3-41).

Figure 3-38. Parallelogram diamonds are commonly named by the angles used to create them. These are 45° angles.

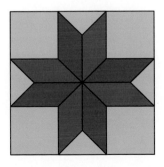

Figure 3-39. Godey's Design is a simple pattern using eight 45° parallelogram diamonds.

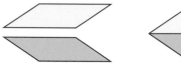

Figure 3-40. These parallelogram diamonds are named for their 30° angles.

Figure 3-41. Cutting Edge is a very dimensional design using 30° diamonds for its inner star. (©1994 Joen Wolfrom)

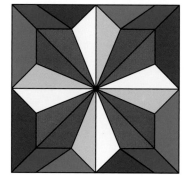

Figure 3-42. Icelandic Poppy uses mirror-imaged obtuse triangles to form its design. Each set of obtuse triangles forms a kite-shaped diamond. (©1994 Joen Wolfrom)

Circles

A circular design in the center of a square quilt can look fantastic. Some of our most gorgeous quilt designs have circular motifs. They are great focal-point designs. The designs radiate from their centers, catching our eyes because of their intriguing designs. Mariner's Compass (Figure 3-43 and Photo 110) is one of our most popular patterns. *Dilly Dahlia* and *Compass Rose* are lovely examples of circular designs (Photos 56 and 76).

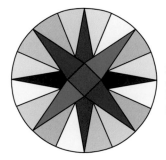

Figure 3-43. Circles can be divided into many parts to create beautiful designs. Mariner's Compass is a popular circular pattern.

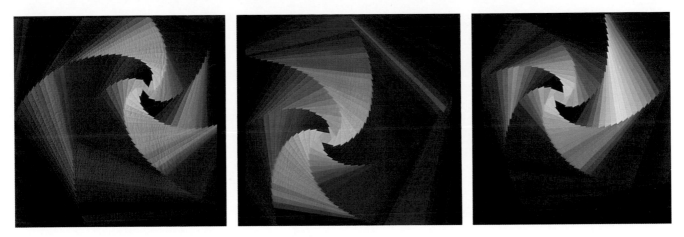

31. REFRACTION 11, 12, 13, 1993, 121" x 39"
Caryl Bryer Fallert, Oswego, Illinois
This contemporary Log Cabin triptych is particularly dynamic because of Caryl's pure color play with value changes. The construction technique is based on traditional Log Cabin piecing; however Caryl used a hexagon format rather than a square. Private collection. Photo: Courtesy of the artist

32. CRUISIN', 1993, 46" x 56"
Janice Ohlson Richards, Vaughn, Washington
The fragile colors of the tint scale are dominant in this quilt, which reflects the beautiful, soft blues of the Caribbean waters as brightly colored fish add contrast. Photo: Ken Wagner

33. CUBIC CARVING, 1994, 66" x 73"
Martie Huston, Santee, California
This is the second in a series of Martie's illusionary quilts showing highlights, shadows, and three-dimensionality. She has used the primary triadic color scheme for her color plan. Sue Atlas, Jane McCabe, and Joyce Baromich also worked on the quilt. Pieced and appliquéd. Photo: Ken Wagner

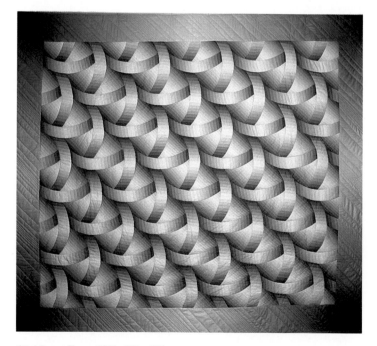

34. MORAL FIBER, 1991, 68" x 62"
Miriam Nathan-Roberts, Berkeley, California
This lustrous, monochromatic design was achieved through subtle value changes within one color family. This design illustrates the principles of repetition, harmony, and unity. Photo: Courtesy of the artist

35. ENTWINING CURVES IN BLOOM, 1989, 56" X 78"
Joen Wolfrom, Fox Island, Washington
Although this quilt uses hues from several color scales, the tint scale is the most dominant. In this free-flowing curved design, Joen uses her free-form freezer-paper technique for piecing. Collection of Ulster Folk and Transport Museum, Northern Ireland. Photo: Ken Wagner

36. WILLIAM TELL'S SON, 1993, 56" x 63"
Designed by Jean Ray Laury, Fresno, California
Jean's wonderful sense of humor comes through in this delightful quilt. Its fun-loving spirit is amplified by the highly contrasting colors. Unity is created through color, shapes, and theme. Sewn by Susan Smeltzer. Photo: Sharon Risedorph, California

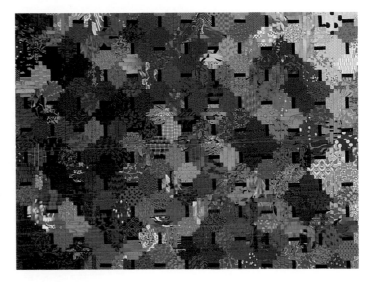

37. FLOWER DRUM SONG, 1990, 31" x 25"
Lesly-Claire Greenberg, Fairfax, Virginia
This unusual Log Cabin design beautifully illustrates the effect warm and cool colors have on each other. The warm yellow colors appear to advance, while the cooler colors seem to recede. Photo: Courtesy of Michele Vernon

38. AMARYLLIS EIGHTH, 60" x 70"
Juanita G. Yeager, Louisville, Kentucky
The warm-colored flowers appear to reach out, as the cooler greens seem to recede quietly into the background. The design, a Dover pattern adaptation of flowers from a stained glass window, is appliquéd. Photo: Ken Wagner

39. NIGHT SHADES, 1993, 48" x 42"
Sandi Cummings, Moraga, California
Night Shades is a quilt filled with visual energy. Besides the high value contrast of the black-and-white check to capture our attention, Sandi has also used yellow as an accent. Machine-quilted by Sandy Klop. Photo: Courtesy of the artist

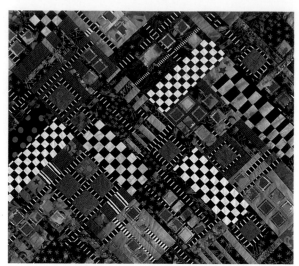

40. TRIBUTE TO TIPPI HEDREN, 1984, 54" x 64"
Janice Ohlson Richards, Vaughn, Washington
Janice visually warmed her blue, violet, and magenta quilt by using the yellows in the sunrise fabrics. This quilt originated from a 10" block. The block was repeated throughout, often being rotated and set in different positions. The swirling quilting lines create the effect of birds flying in the wind. Photo: Ken Wagner

41. THE LODGE OF TRUE REFLECTION, 1994, 69" x 52"
Janice Ohlson Richards, Vaughn, Washington
This original pieced picture was inspired by the view from Janice's family cabin window. The nighttime hues incorporate the deep, dark colors of the cool shades. Photo: Ken Wagner

42. SOUTHWEST OF AMISH
1994, 58" x 66"
Anna Edwards, Danville, California
Anna uses many deep, warm shades. She is fascinated with the culture, art, and traditions of Indians, our first Americans. Thus, this quilt celebrates their life. Photo: Ken Wagner

43. BLUEBERRY HILL
1986, 72" x 84"
Carol Ann Wadley, Temple, Texas
This wonderful double-bed sized quilt was created using the traditional Maple Leaf pattern in an innovative setting. The autumn leaves are made from hues in the warm side of the shade color scale. Private collection. Photo: Sue Stearns

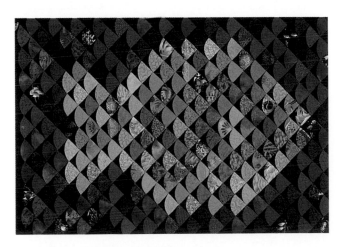

44. TROPICAL FISH, 1993, 69" x 58"
Nancy S. Breland, Pennington, New Jersey
The design for this fascinating quilt emerged as Nancy placed quarter circles of fabric on her design wall. The fish is created primarily through value changes. Intensity changes add intrigue. Photo: Jay Turkel, New Jersey

45. ISLAND GIRL
1991, 55" x 43"
Linda S. Schmidt, Dublin, California
This beautifully subtle quilt created in the tone scale is an interpretation of a photograph Linda took of her daughter. Strip-piecing, curved piecing, and appliqué were used to create this picture. Photo: Ken Wagner

46. LADIES OF THE BOARD, 1990, 68" x 40"
Janice Ohlson Richards, Vaughn, Washington
The subtle tone scale was used for the majority of this story quilt, as it reflected Janice's father's aging millwork company. By changing the color scale, our eyes immediately focus on the three sisters. Three traditional blocks, Attic Window, Boardroom, and Millwheel, were incorporated in the background design. Photo: Ken Wagner

Adding the Visual Giants—Color and Value

NATURE AND ITS COLOR SCALES

For thousands of years, nature has beautifully colored our earth; it has devised methods to categorize colors and set up wonderful color schemes with which to work. For as long as man has been involved in art, nature has been used as a color study. We, too, would do well to use nature as a major guide to help us create beautiful quilts. So as you watch a sunset, gaze at an exquisite rose, or contemplate the arrival of a fresh day, study the colors in a new light.

All colors in the world can be divided into four main groups. These divisions are easy to understand because they follow the same pattern as the seasons of the year. These four seasonal color divisions are called *color scales*. This organizational system of scales is closely related to musical scales. Musical scales organize notes into a workable system for the musician, while color scales organize the myriad of colors that surround us. These four color scales are pure colors, tints, shades, and tones.

The Spirited Pure Colors

The brightest colors in our world belong to the *pure color scale*. The blazing sun, summer's green lawn, a juicy orange, the cerulean blue of the midday sky, royal purple ceremonial robes, a crispy red apple, the brilliant reddish-purple fuchsia—these represent colorful members of the

Figure 4-1. The brilliant flowers of summer are examples of the dynamic pure color scale. This is the most spirited scale of the four color groups. Photo by the author

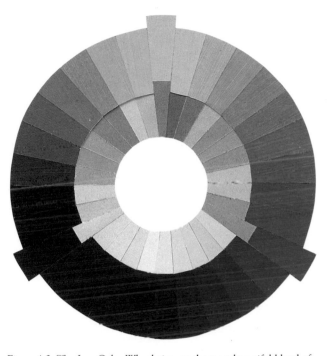

Figure 4-2. The Ives Color Wheel gives us the most beautiful blend of hues from which to work. The primaries are magenta, yellow, and turquoise. Artist: Judith Buskirk. Photo: Ken Wagner

pure color scale. Our most brilliant flowers put on a display of pure colors in the summer months (Figure 4-1).

The most widely known members of the pure scale are the *primary colors*. All other pure colors are created by combining two of the three primary colors together. Primary colors, along with all their offspring hues, are considered pure colors because their strength has not been diluted in any way. Most of us were taught in school that primary colors are color-crayon red, blue, and yellow. If you have ever mixed colors using these primaries, you know they result in somewhat muddy colors, lacking vibrance and clarity. Therefore, fabric makers and printing companies use the Ives Color Wheel (Figure 4-2). The three primary colors in this wheel are magenta, turquoise (cyan), and yellow. They create magnificent colors when mixed.

Magenta, turquoise, and yellow are the parent colors to the most dynamic, brilliant hues to meet our eyes. The most commonly known pure colors are yellow, yellow-green, green, blue-green, blue, periwinkle, blue-violet, violet, purple, magenta, red, red-orange, orange, and yellow-orange.

Pure colors are considered the hues of summer. Their strength produces a dynamic presentation. They create a mood of happiness and spirit. Quilts using pure colors as their dominant scale are definite eye-catchers (Photos 36, 38, and 105). *Refraction 11, 12, 13* (Photo 31) is magnificent in its use of pure color. If you enjoy strong colors, consider using hues from this scale.

The Gentle Tint Scale

Visually, the *tint scale* colors give the opposite effect from the pure hues. Tints are the softest, most fragile colors in our world. They range from the soft blush-white hues (tinged with a soft color) to those hues only slightly lighter than their pure color. The majority of tints lies somewhere between these two extremes.

Figure 4-3 The soft, gentle tint hues are often shown in the garden's springtime flowers. Photo by the author

If you want your quilt to reflect the mood or theme of spring, these are the colors that should dominate throughout your quilt (Figure 4-3). Also, tints are very useful for creating several illusions. In particular, opalescence, luster, and luminosity can all be attained using tints. The best-recognized tints are apricot, soft yellow, cream, powder blue, mint green, peach, pink, lavender, and robin's-egg blue. White is the most appropriate neutral to use when working with tints, because all tints are made from white.

Quilts that chiefly use the tint scale are usually subtle. Often, they are not noticed from a distance. Their pleasure is savored in close viewing. Unfortunately, tint fabrics are difficult to find in the marketplace, so few quilts are actually created with this as the dominant scale. Examples of quilts using tints in their design are *Cruisin'* (Photo 32) and *Entwining Curves in Bloom* (Photo 35).

The Shade Scale's Dual Personality

Colors in the *shade scale* have had black added to them. Some shades have been slightly blackened, so they are only a bit darker than their pure color parent. Others are so dark, they appear almost black. The natural neutral to use with shades is black, because all shades are created by adding black. This scale has two very distinct personalities: the warm shades and the cool shades.

THE WARM SHADES

When black is added to warm colors (*e.g.*, yellow-green, yellow, orange, orange-red), the hues change drastically. Most transform themselves into fall hues (Figure 4-4). Their autumnal appearance is seen in great glory when the leaves turn rust, brown, olive, russet, avocado, copper, burnt orange, and pumpkin in fall. Quilts using the rich warm shades include *Cupid's Dart* (Photo 8) and *Southwest of Amish* (Photo 42).

If you want to make an autumn quilt, in theme or subtle imagery, the warmly shaded hues are the color choice for you. You may add hues from other scales, but the majority of your colors will come from the shade scale. The other hues act as accents or backdrops. *September Mountain* (Photo 84) and *Blueberry Hill* (Photo 43) use the autumn colors and theme for their dominant imageries.

Figure 4-4. Leaves changing color are the first signs of autumn. Warm colors that have been blackened are autumnal in nature. Photo by the author

Figure 4-5. The night hues come from the cool side of the shade color scale. Deep, dark colors from this scale have had black added to them. Photo by the author

Figure 4-6. Tones are colors that have been visually grayed. They are often soft, subtle, or misty. To create a quilt reflecting winter's mood or imagery, tones need to be used. Photo by the author

THE COOL SHADES

On the other side of the color wheel, the hues appear cool. These include green, blue-green, blue, blue-violet, and violet. When black has been added to these colors, they become deep, rich hues, appropriate for sea, night-time, and deep forest imagery (Figure 4-5). Their most familiar members are navy, forest green, deep ultra-marine blue, maroon, and plum. Richly colored shade quilts from the cool side include *Chroma III: Vinifera* (Photo 63) and *The Lodge of True Reflection* (Photo 41). Note that the lodge presents a strong contrast in this nighttime scene.

Additionally, the deep, dark shades can be used as the background coloration for iridescence. Their richness becomes a wonderful contrast to the bright pure colors used for the flickers of iridescence.

The Subtle Tones

The remaining colors in our world fall into the *tone scale*. This is an immense group of colors. Tones are colors that have been visually grayed. They include beige, tan, taupe, mauve, heather, slate blue, and sage green. This is the scale most widely used by quiltmakers.

A tone can be as light as any tint, or as dark as any shade. However, its chief characteristic is that it appears to be grayed. When we say that a color has been toned down, we imply that it has been grayed. Since gray is prevalent in all toned fabric, it is the most natural neutral to use with a toned quilt.

Tones are the hues of winter. If you want to make a winter scene or create a winter imagery quilt, use colors from the tone scale (Figure 4-6). Tones offer subtle beauty rather than drama. These quilts are often very calming (Photos 45 and 71). *Rondo Veneziano* a subtly toned design, is elegant with understated beauty (Photo 19).

Tones are useful for a great many illusions. If you want to create depth, mist, fog, or an ethereal effect, you must use tones (Photo 1 on page 9; Photos 24, 73, 74, 75, and 91). The illusions of luminosity (Photos 2, 25, and 93) and opalescence (Photo 23) also need toned hues. Sometimes toned hues are used to create luster or shadows (Photos 25, 34, and 79). Tones, then, play a very important role when we create visual illusions.

Tints, pure colors, and shades may be used as accents in a tone-scale artwork. Because colors from other scales react strongly when placed in a toned quilt, this must be done with great care. Usually our eyes end up focusing on the colors from another scale, so it must be our intention to draw attention to this non-toned area.

In Janice Richards' *The Ladies of the Board* (Photo 46), the ladies' figures were done in the brightest colors, while the rest of the design was created in extremely subdued hues. Janice wanted the ladies to stand out. Her use of a different scale draws our eyes immediately to the ladies. If she had not intended this, a change of scale could have been a distraction.

Sometimes it appears difficult to tell the difference between a deep, rich shade and an extremely dark-toned fabric. A true shade has clean, crisp coloring, while a tone appears veiled and unclear.

COLOR FAMILIES

Every pure color is the parent to an almost limitless array of tints, shades, and tones. We call this large group of related hues a *color family*. For instance, the periwinkle (blue-violet) family of hues includes every tint, shade, and tone possible, as well as the pure color.

INTENSITY

The most intense colors are the pure hues (Figures 4-1 and 4-2). As a pure color is diluted by adding black, white, gray, or another hue, its brilliance is affected. It becomes less intense; it no longer has the vivid clarity of its pure form. In the context of this book, a color is considered less intense when it has been visually grayed or toned.

Pure yellow is intense; beige, a grayed yellow, is not intense. Rose, a grayed hue, is of low intensity; fuchsia, a pure color, is clearly intense. In art, an intense color may be referred to as fully saturated. Thus a royal blue is intense or fully saturated. Slate blue, in contrast, is low in saturation, or low in intensity, because it has been grayed. *Refraction 11, 12, and 13* (Photo 31) is intense, or fully saturated; the quilts in Photos 45 and 46 have low intensity or saturation because their colors are very toned.

COLOR DOMINANCE

When you design your quilt, it is very important to choose one color family to be visually dominant. If you want to create a quilt with periwinkle, green, purple, and creamy apricot, you must decide which of these colors will play the dominant role. After determining the lead color, choose the secondary color and the accent colors. If you are indecisive about this, the colors may compete with each other, causing confusion or distraction.

COLOR TEMPERATURES

Colors often appear either cool or warm. We think of yellow, orange, and red as warm, while green, blue, and violet are considered cool. However, all colors can appear to be warm or cool, depending on nearby colors.

Most colors can appear either cool or warm, if they are carefully placed in the design. A teal will look warm next to a color that has less yellow in its makeup. Thus, when teal and navy are placed together, the teal will react as a warm color. Likewise, a red can appear cool, if it is placed next to another red that has more yellow in its makeup. So two reds, a blued red and an orange-red, placed side-by-side, can give the illusion of both warmth and coolness. One will recede while the other pulls forward.

If you want a color to appear cooler than it actually is, place it next to an obviously warm color; likewise, if you want a color to appear warmer than it is, surround it with cool colors (Photos 58 and 126). White almost always appears cool. So tints, whether they are yellow, orange, or blue, reflect coolness (Photo 32). Black is considered a warm color.

Warm colors excite us. They can make us feel warmer than we actually are. They attract attention dramatically. Warm hues tend to advance, especially when surrounded by cool colors (Photos 78, 79, and 80). In contrast, cool colors have a calming effect. They may even make us feel colder than we actually are. Cool colors generally recede into the background, especially when warm colors are present (Photos 37 and 38). You can promote the illusion of depth by contrasting warm colors with cool colors. Good examples of warm and cool contrasting colors include quilts created by Gail Biddle (Photo 65) and Erika Odemer (Photo 58).

Velda Newman has achieved wonderful results by positioning the warm hues in the background of *Hydrangea* (Photo 47). Through her thoughtful use of color, she has also created depth, highlights, and shadows.

COLOR AND VALUE

Although we respond intensely to color, we are just as profoundly affected by how light or how dark colors are. We are so sensitive to light (or darkness) that it most assuredly affects our personalities, our emotions, and even our physical activities. This darkness or lightness in colors is called *value*. Colors close to white are considered *high-valued colors* (Figure 4-7). Colors close to black are *low-valued colors* (Figure 4-5). Colors that fall in the middle range are considered *middle-valued colors*.

Figure 4-7. Colors close to white are considered high in value. They are usually soft, delicate hues. Most tints are considered high-valued colors. Photo by the author

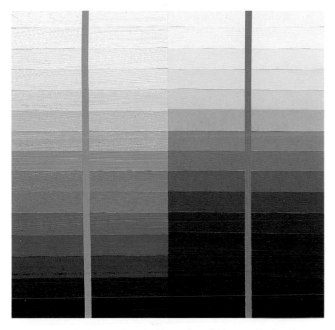

Figure 4-8. Colors move from highest values (lightest colors) to lowest values (darkest colors). The rose and neutral gray narrow vertical strips appear to change values as they move from the top of the scale to the bottom, although they remain the same color. Artist: Judith Buskirk. Photo by Ken Wagner

Most tints, light tones, and the lightest pure colors (*e.g.*, yellow, yellow-orange, yellow-green) are considered high-valued. The darkest colors of the shade scale, the tone scale, and the darkest pure colors (*e.g.*, violet, purple) are low-valued hues. Middle-valued colors include some pure colors (*e.g.*, blue-green, orange-red) and those colors that appear neither dark nor light.

Values are like stairsteps going from the darkest hue to the lightest (Figure 4-8). The darkest colors are at the bottom of the stairs, while the highest steps are the lightest in value. The low-valued hues give the most weight, acting like an anchor, while the highest-valued colors are airy and fantasy-like, seeming to float above all else.

Colors are very sensitive to values. They react differently, depending on where they are placed in the design. What appears to be a dark color in one part of your quilt may seem quite light elsewhere; it may all but disappear in another part of your quilt. Color values play an extremely important part in our quilts.

Look at the two value scales (Figure 4-8). The narrow, vertical strips in these scales are made from the middle-valued pink and gray of each value scale. Notice how the strips look really dark when next to the highest-valued tints and tones; additionally, the colors look extremely light against the darkest shades and tones. The strips seem to lose themselves in the middle part of the value scale. Visually, it doesn't seem possible these two color strips are the same color throughout.

This example is a marvelous illustration of how colors appear differently when put in dissimilar surroundings. Don't discard a particular fabric from your quilt just because it does not work in one area. Move it around to see if it looks better in a different position. Also, just because you think a fabric should work in a particular place does not mean that it will. Don't keep a fabric in your quilt if its value is distracting.

Value Key

The relative value of art is often described as a key. Thus, art may be *high-keyed* (primarily light, high-value colors), *middle-keyed* (mostly middle-value colors), or *low-keyed* (predominantly dark, low-value colors). Each artwork should be created with one key emphasized. Each of us is drawn to one key. Know which key you prefer.

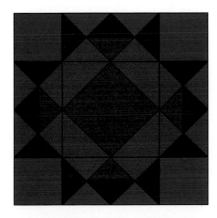

Figure 4-9. When no value contrast is present, the design can disappear. This happens regardless of the value key used.

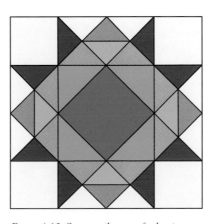

Figure 4-10. Some quilters prefer having a limited amount of value contrast in their work. In high-valued art, this creates a soft, subtle effect.

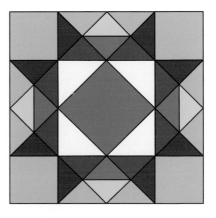

Figure 4-11. Strong value contrasts are not necessary to make an effective design. Make certain, however, enough value contrast exists to allow the design to be well seen.

Figure 4-12. Nature often uses strongly contrasting colors together. The visual result can be dynamic. If you use strongly contrasting colors together, make certain one is visually dominant. Photo by the author

Values and Contrast

Many quilts lack value contrast. This makes the design difficult to discern (Figure 4-9). It is disappointing to finish a quilt and find the design either fails to show, or the wrong part of the design pulls out. To keep this from happening, you must be aware of how you are going to use values to promote your design. Make certain there is some contrast in your values. This value contrast does not have to be extreme (Figures 4-10 and 4-11).

Nancy Breland's *Tropical Fish* (Photo 44) is quite successful. She carefully manipulated the values in her fabric placement so the design would appear. If Nancy had placed the different value scales haphazardly throughout her quilt, her design would have been indistinguishable.

If you like strongly contrasting designs, use dark and light colors together (Photos 109 and 110). Nature has examples of highly contrasting values in many summer flowers (Figure 4-12). Be certain, however, that one of the values is dominant. For instance, the quilt should be visually darker or lighter in its design. When strong colors are used in equal amounts, they fight each other for visual dominance. This can become extremely distracting.

If your quilt is primarily created in high values, or light colors, use one or more middle-valued colors to add needed contrast (Photos 95 and 96). These can be used as accents. If you are making a quilt in low-valued colors, or dark colors, definitely consider adding contrast by incorporating a few middle-valued hues or some high-valued accents (Photo 44). If you only use very dark colors in your quilt, again, the design will be lost (Figure 4-9).

When working with middle-valued colors, you have three ways to add contrast. You may include a few high-valued hues; you may move down the value scale to include darker hues. Or, you may choose to use both high- and low-valued colors for your contrast. Some quilts are stunning blends of colors, ranging from high to low. Caryl Fallert's *Refraction 11, 12, and 13* (Photo 31) is such an example.

Color Schemes

There are five major color schemes to consider when planning your quilts. Each scheme uses colors differently; each has its own advantages and visual strengths. All of these color schemes are seen readily in nature. If you are uncomfortable about choosing colors for your quilt, work within these parameters.

Do not feel you must confine yourself to these color schemes in order to make a beautiful quilt. As you gain experience, you may only use them as a reference, as the more you work with color, the more intuitively you will work.

Monochromatic Color Scheme

Monochromatic is the most sophisticated of all color schemes. Its simplistic beauty is based on using only one color family to achieve its design. Nature uses this scheme liberally (Figure 4-13). These colors can include tints, tones, shades, and the pure color within the family. Depending on the color used, the design can be very calming (Photo 34) or extremely exciting.

Figure 4-13. The monochromatic color scheme is the most sophisticated of all color plans. Its simplistic beauty is based on using only one color family to achieve its design. Photo by the author

For success, value change is usually the most important design element in a monochromatic color scheme. The design also may be created through intensity changes. Therefore, a monochromatic design uses colors from the same family, either contrasting darkness with lightness, or grayness against pureness or brilliancy. The amount of contrast in value or intensity is up to you.

If you find a monochromatically colored quilt lacks interest or seems monotonous, look closely at the fabrics used. The problem most likely lies in the lack of value or intensity change. These contrasts are essential to creating the monochromatic color scheme. Try making stronger value or intensity contrasts than you currently have, if you see this as a problem.

If you have too many non-related, highly contrasting values in your design, it can be distracting in a monochromatic color scheme. Our eyes don't know where to rest, so they jump around, leaving us uncomfortable. If you are working with highly contrasting values, and they are visually disjointed, rearrange them so they move the eyes across the quilt design. Also, make certain one value key is dominant.

The Harmonic Analogous Color Scheme

The analogous color scheme uses colors that lie side by side on the color wheel. Generally, this works best with three color families. It is an extremely beautiful color scheme because there is such harmony between the colors. Nature uses this scheme as gradation steps from one color to another (Figures 2-10 and 4-14). We also can use the beautiful, related gradation steps to create our own designs. The analogous color scheme can be restful, particularly if the closely related colors are cool (Photo 63). Other examples of analogous designs include Photos 49, 54, 55, and 121; and Photo 138 on page 144.

Figure 4-14. The analogous color scheme uses colors that lie side by side on the color wheel. It is extremely beautiful because there is such harmony between the colors. Nature uses this scheme as gradation steps from one color to another. Photo by the author

Examples of the analogous color scheme are (1) green, blue-green, turquoise; (2) turquoise, blue, violet; (3) purple, magenta, red; (4) magenta, red, orange; and (5) orange, yellow-orange, and yellow. It is also possible to create an analogous color scheme with colors that encompass a larger color grouping, such as red, orange, and yellow, or yellow, green, and blue.

Closely related colors work particularly well with each other. Their interacting clashing potential can create stunning brilliance (Photo 61). Even quite grayed or subdued colors are enhanced by a flowing richness when placed with adjacent colors (Photo 69).

SELECTING THE ROLES FOR YOUR COLORS

After you have picked the adjacent colors you want to use (usually three color families), select the dominant, the secondary, and the accent color families. While creating, remember the role each is to play as you work. Certain hues may attempt to usurp the power from the dominant color family, so be aware of this possibility.

The Complementary Color Scheme

In the complementary color scheme, opposite colors on the color wheel are used (Figure 4-2). Often this color scheme is illustrated in books with opposing orange and blue circles, yellow and violet circles, or red and green circles. Many of us have avoided using this particular color scheme because it seems so garish. However, the real beauty of the complementary color scheme is not in its two pure hues, but in the intermixing of those two colors. Glorious colors are created in this scheme when two complementary hues are delicately blended together.

It is almost impossible to know what these color interminglings will be without experimenting with paint or watercolor pencils. If you are interested in working in this color scheme, play with paints first. Swirl one complementary paint color into the other (e.g., violet into yellow). You will be fascinated by the colors created. Likewise, if you blend the second color into the first (e.g., yellow into violet), the beauty of these colors is also magnificent. The range of these colors can be multiplied greatly by tinting, toning, or shading these blended hues.

THE VISUAL EFFECTS OF THE MAJOR PARTNERS

Although there are many complementary partners to choose from, the three most prominent are yellow and violet (Figure 4-15), turquoise (blue) and orange (Figure 4-16), and magenta (red) and green (Figure 4-17). Each has its own unique visual effect.

Figure 4-15. Yellow and violet (purple) combine the lightest and darkest hues on the color wheel. This combination of colors best promotes the imagery of highlights and shadows. Photo by the author

Figure 4-17. Red (or magenta) and green are equal in value, so you must be careful to make one more visually dominant than the other. Pink, rose, or other less intense forms of red and magenta are not so prone to competing. Photo by the author

The yellow and violet partnership combines the darkest and lightest hues on the color wheel. This partnership usually is not as intense as the other two major partners. It is a combination of colors that gives us the imagery of highlights and shadows. With yellow being the brightest color, it will dominate in this partnership unless you work hard to change it. You can do this by either shading or toning the yellow greatly, or by limiting its presence. Also, you can enhance violet as the dominant partner by keeping it as intense as possible, or using lighter values.

Orange and blue are not only opposite on the color wheel, but also they elicit the extremes of hot and cold (Photo 111 on page 116). Orange, in its most intense form, can easily overpower turquoise (blue), as it is almost twice as bright. Thus, orange will always be the dominant color unless you work to weaken its role. To calm orange,

lessen its intensity by toning it. You can also shade or tint it, if that works within your design. To make turquoise (blue) the dominant hue, pure orange must be used sparsely or be greatly changed from its pure form. Changing the orange to rust or brown calms the color greatly (Photo 53).

Pure magenta and green are almost equal in value. Because these two readily compete with each other for visual dominance, you must be especially careful to make one more powerful than the other. Do not leave this decision to chance. Unfortunately, this often happens when working with green and red winter holiday projects.

Remember, if you are working in the complementary color scheme and your colors are too harsh, use more grayed-down fabrics (tones). One color must always play the dominant role. If the partners compete visually for this prime role, it leads to visual discomfort for the viewer. If this is a problem, lessen the use of the secondary color or weaken its intensity throughout the design.

Figure 4-16. Blue and orange are not only opposite on the color wheel, they also elicit the extremes of hot and cold. Orange, in its most intense form, can easily overpower turquoise, as it is almost twice as bright. Thus, orange will always be the dominant color unless you work to weaken its role, as is done in *Serenity at Dawn* by the author. Photo: Ken Wagner

Figure 4-18. The split-complementary color scheme allows for a temperature shift. Here, the analogous colors of yellow, yellow-orange, and orange are signalling the last minutes of a sunset, as the blue-violet sky (the complement of yellow-orange) becomes a more dominant force. Photo by the author

The Split-Complementary Color Scheme

The split-complementary color scheme is actually two color schemes brought together as one. It combines the analogous color scheme with the complementary color scheme (Figure 4-18). This results in four color families being part of this arrangement. It is a very beautiful, harmonious color plan with a blend of warm and cool colors (Photos 40 and 96).

To use the split-complementary color scheme, first choose three analogous colors. The fourth color is always determined by the middle analogous color. Its complementary partner becomes the fourth hue. If the three analogous hues are magenta, red, and orange, the fourth color is blue-green, red's complement. If they are magenta, violet, and blue, the fourth hue is yellow (Photo 70).

This is a very exciting color scheme to work in, because it is so versatile. Naturally, you have to choose the dominant color, the secondary color, and the accents. Any of the four colors can be chosen for the dominant hue. Usually the most difficult color to use as the dominant one is the complementary color. Doreen Thompson was very successful in accomplishing this with her quilt (Photo 60).

If the complementary color happens to be yellow, or a similarly bright, warm color, the task is not quite so difficult.

Each of the four colors may include tints, shades, and tones. While creating, don't lose sight of which color is dominant. Attempt to move the colors across the composition, so your eyes are led from one area to the next (Photo 70).

The Triadic Color Scheme

The triadic color scheme uses any three colors that are of equal distance from each other on the color wheel (Figure 4-2). On a 12-step color wheel, the colors in a triad would include every fourth color. The most common triadic color schemes are (1) the primary triad (yellow, turquoise, and magenta); (2) the secondary triad (green, violet, and orange (Figure 4-19); and (3) the two tertiary triads (yellow-green, blue, and red, and the combination of blue-green, purple, and yellow-orange) (Figure 4-19).

As with the complementary color scheme, the beauty of using the triads is not in working with the three strong pure colors. Instead, its strength lies in the gorgeous intermingling that happens as the three colors are mixed. If you are interested in using this triadic plan, use paints or colored pencils to find the blending colors of the specific triad you have chosen. Examples of quilts using this scheme include those in photos 31 and 33.

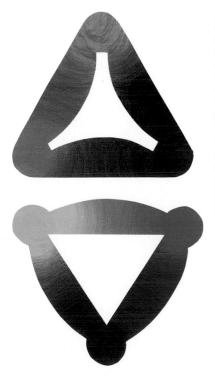

Figure 4-19. The triadic color scheme uses any three colors that are an equal distance from each other on the color wheel. The secondary triad is green, violet, and orange (above), while the tertiary triad uses the combination of blue-green, purple, and yellow-orange (below). Illustration by Judith Buskirk, Gig Harbor, Washington. Photo: Ken Wagner

Using Accents in Your Color Schemes

If an accent color is surrounded by colors that are very similar to it, the accent will be less dramatic in effect than if it has strong contrast. An intense color chosen to be the accent in your quilt should never compete for dominance. If its impact gives it too much visual strength in the design, lessen the amount of its use, or exchange it for a fabric less pure in color.

The dominant color retains the visual strength. Yellow is often chosen as an accent (Photo 39). Since yellow is the brightest and strongest of all colors, it can easily succeed in accidentally taking over the dominant role. Therefore, care must be taken when using yellow. In contrast, violet, even in its purest stage, is too dark to draw much attention to itself when used as an accent.

For a more detailed discussion about color and color illusions, refer to *The Magical Effects of Color* by the author (see Sources).

ACTIVITIES AND EXTENDED LEARNING:

1. Using quilts in this text, notice if there is a relationship between values and the quilts you are strongly drawn to and those you do not care for.

2. Using quilt magazines and books, find several quilts that fit into each of the color schemes. After doing this, do you find you have a preference for one particular color scheme?

3. Analyze the quilts created in the monochromatic color scheme. What do you notice is the difference between the successful and unsuccessful monochromatic quilts? How does the quiltmaker attract your attention within the quilt (how does she achieve her focus)?

4. If you are interested in working with the complementary color scheme, work first with paint to find the wonderful colors created by the partner's intermixing. Purchase Liquitex™ Acrylic Paints (liquid or tube) in your selected colors. With an inexpensive small brush, swirl one color into the other. Experiment as much as you can. (*Note:* Paint from tubes should be watered down in an open container. Make its consistency similar to that of frosting.)

47. HYDRANGEA, 1989, 99" x 84"
Velda E. Newman, Nevada City, California
This awesome quilt is created in large scale, allowing us to better appreciate the delicate petals of
the much-loved hydrangea blossoms. Magnifying its size allows us to view it in a different perspective
than normally seen. Velda's play with highlights and shadows is superbly done. Appliquéd. Photo:
Stephen R. Solinsky, California

48. GERANIUM
1993, 98" x 80"
Velda E. Newman,
Nevada City, California
Velda masterfully creates large-scale art quilts. She adds intrigue by surprising us with a magnification of her design theme. This exaggeration of size leaves us spellbound by both nature's intricacies and her ability to reproduce them so beautifully. Pieced and appliquéd. Photo: Stephen R. Solinsky, California

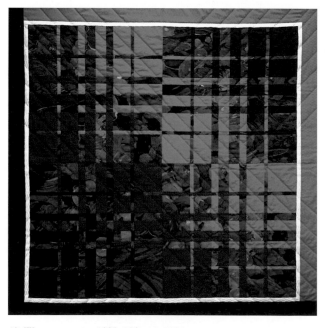

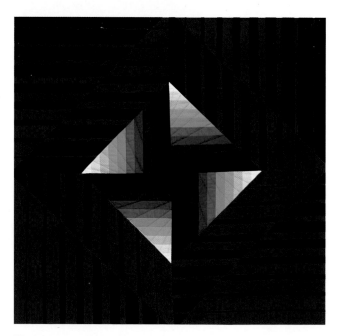

49. WINTERGARTEN, 1990, 113CM X 113CM
Regula Nussbaumer, St. Gallen, Switzerland
This subtle design creates its pattern through repetition, harmony, unity, and contrast. The size of the quilt complements the scale of the design. *Wintergarten* has been created in an analogous color scheme. Photo: Courtesy of the artist

50. AUFBRUCH, 1990, 112CM X 112CM
Regula Nussbaumer, St. Gallen, Switzerland
Aufbruch creates interest through repetition, harmony, unity, and contrast. The scale of the design works well with its overall size. Photo: Courtesy of the artist

Proportion and Scale

When scale or proportion seems out of balance in a design, it bothers our visual senses—even if we do not know what is wrong or why we feel discomfort. If a quilt or other art appears beautiful, we rarely think of proportion or scale. It is only when these elements are blatantly incorrect that we become aware of their significance.

PROPORTION

Proportion deals with the size of shapes within a design. We want our shapes to be in proportion to one another. Sometimes one shape is out of proportion with the rest of the shapes in a design. It may be too large or too small in comparison to the other shapes.

Proportion may be best explained with the following analogies: A dinner-plate dahlia is much too large to be placed together in an arrangement with a miniature rose; the latter would be lost in such a bouquet. The dahlia needs to stand on its own or be placed with flowers of its own size and visual strength; likewise, the small rose needs flowers that are nearer its size for a successful display. Along the same line, elegant tall gladioli are out of proportion to their vase if they are placed in a small container (Figure 5-1). The result is a flower bouquet that looks like it is about ready to topple. It needs to be in a vase that coincides with its height (Figure 5-2).

PROPORTION AND TRADITIONAL QUILT PATTERNS

Proportion is an important element in all art, even quiltmaking. In a design, when any shape is out of proportion to the others, the eye automatically is drawn to it. Fortunately, most traditional quilt patterns are designed

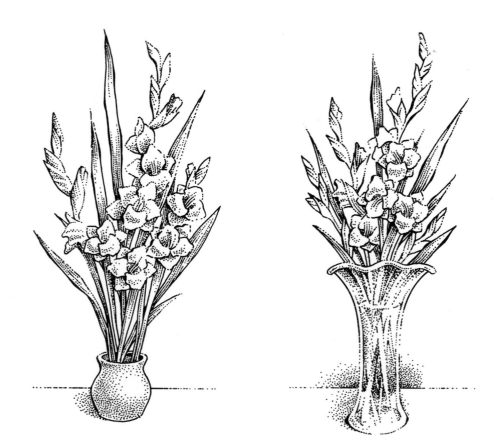

Figure 5-1. (left). Using a small vase for an elegant, tall bouquet of gladioli makes the flowers look ungainly in their setting. The vase is out of proportion to the stately, long flowers. Their proportional disagreement causes distraction.

Figure 5-2. (right). By using a vase that is in proportion to the size of the gladioli bouquet, visual balance is achieved.

Figure 5-3. This mansion placed on a tiny plot of land overwhelms the property. The scale of the house is wrong for the size of the land. Additionally, the entrance, fence, and shrubbery are out of proportion to the mansion as they are too small to be in visual agreement. Artwork can have the same problems if scale and proportion are not addressed.

Figure 5-4. This tiny cottage placed on enormous, sprawling grounds is dwarfed by its surroundings. The focus is too small for the area provided. Additionally, the entry is out of proportion to the home. It overwhelms the small abode.

with their various shapes proportionate to each other. Rarely do they need changing. There are times, however, when proportion becomes a problem in a quilt. It is important for us to recognize these times, so we can make the appropriate changes.

The most frequent occurrence of incorrect proportion happens when borders are added to the quilt top. Specifically, if the border shapes are larger than the inside shapes, visual disharmony occurs. Our eyes are drawn immediately to the border. This results in visual competition between the two sections, rather than the border enhancing the design. If you create new shapes for your border, make certain they are in proportion to the other shapes.

Proportion may also be jeopardized when two structurally non-related block patterns are put together in one design. Related blocks do not usually have this problem, because their shapes are comparable. For instance, two nine-patch patterns will use shapes with similar sizes. However, when you combine a nine-patch pattern with an eight-pointed star design, the sizes of the various shapes may be different enough to cause visual disturbance. If this happens, the shapes are probably not in proportion to each other. You must then evaluate your block partners and consider changing one of them.

Assessing and Alleviating the Problem

In most block designs, shapes relate well to each other. They have good visual interaction. However, if a certain shape pulls out and overwhelms the design, this shape is too large for the setting. The best way to eliminate this kind of proportional problem is to break the overly large shape into smaller pieces.

Occasionally you can compensate for a shape's size by exceptionally fine fabric selection. You may even make your own fabric by combining many different materials. This tends to break up the large surface. When a solid-colored fabric is used in an out-of-proportion shape, the problem is accentuated. The shape must be divided even more, or interesting fabric placement must be made.

Purposely Making Disproportionate Shapes

You may wish to purposely exaggerate the size of one or more shapes, thereby making it out of proportion to the other shapes. If you do this, care should be taken so that the exaggeration is clearly understood. Excitement or intrigue results. An example of exaggeration has been created by Shawn Levy (Photo 134).

Figure 5-5. By placing the mansion in a setting that allows it to breathe, the mansion no longer overwhelms the space. With the scale appropriate and the landscaping in proportion, the mansion takes on a look of grand elegance. Art, too, needs to have both scale and proportion in visual agreement to allow it to reach its fullest potential.

Figure 5-6. The tiny cottage placed on a small plot of land looks charmingly cozy. The scale is correct. With the walkway, fence, and shrubbery diminished in size, the parts of the setting are in proportion to each other. Art must work in the same manner, with scale and proportion in visual agreement.

SCALE

Scale refers to the relationship between an artistic composition and its total size. If an artwork is out-of-scale, our desire for beauty is disturbed. The design may be too small for the total size. With regard to quilts, if an error is made, it usually means the design composition has not been given enough room to develop its full potential. The total size is too small for the design.

Scale can easily be explained through an analogy: A mansion placed on a tiny plot of land, or a tiny cottage surrounded by huge gardens and park lands, are both visually disconcerting (Figures 5-3 and 5-4). They are both out-of-scale with their surroundings. A stately, large residence situated in a tightly contained area will appear squeezed or constrained. It has no room to breathe. With its strength of design and large size, a mansion is best served by expansive lawns, gardens, and treed areas surrounding it. Likewise, the tiny cottage becomes visually lost when placed in the middle of an immense lawn, gardens, and treed borders. It does not have the visual presence to hold the components together. The cottage is visually overwhelmed by its surroundings. It needs to be nestled snugly on a small piece of property.

Each has its own sense of scale. When scale is wisely utilized, the cottage will be enchantingly lovely; the mansion will be magnificently beautiful (Figures 5-5 and 5-6). When this element is ignored, visual beauty is lessened or destroyed for both.

As in the example of the cottage and the mansion, we must consider what amount of space will be best for our particular design. Some designs need confinement, while others require lots of room to evolve.

Aufbruch (Photo 50) is a striking design that needs very little space to tell its story. If it were a huge quilt, the design would not be nearly as successful. *Wintergarten* (Photo 49) is also visually pleasing as a small piece. With both, the scale works very well.

USING YOUR INTUITIVE DESIGN STYLE

Although there is an assumed standard for creating a design with proper proportion and scale, your own unique design style must become a factor in your work. Through experience, you will find your own method of dealing with proportion and scale. The way you work will be considered a part of your design style. This individuality is what makes art so interesting and exciting. *Forest Flowing* (Photo 69) is one such example. Before working in an exaggerated scale, it is wise to understand the concepts of proportion and scale. This will give you greater success.

An artist may feel compelled to create quilt art that uses extremely large shapes. This automatically dictates a larger total surface area so the design can develop. Velda Newman is one quilt artist who masterfully creates awesome artwork in large scale. Her pieces are immense. They are particularly wonderful to see when you can stand back 30 feet or more. Two examples of her work include *Hydrangea* (Photo 47) and *Geranium* (Photo 48).

WORKING WITH SCALE— LETTING YOUR DESIGN DICTATE SIZE

When a quilt's design appears awkward, the problem often lies in the design having been stopped too soon. It wasn't allowed the space to develop to its full potential. Sadly, this design problem is quite prevalent in our field. This is particularly common in innovative and contemporary quilts. Perhaps we are so anxious to have the work finished, we ignore the design's flow.

If we take care to watch our design evolve as we work, we might see that it calls for more surface design than we had originally planned. Perhaps adding one or two more rows of blocks will make the difference between an acceptable quilt and a dynamic quilt. Try not to compromise the design in your eagerness to finish the quilt. Be willing to consider developing the design further than you had anticipated.

Rethinking the Design Potential

When I began exploring contemporary design, I notoriously stopped my designs before they were ready. *Changing Times* (Photo 111 on page 116) had the potential to be an interesting quilt. However, I cut it off before it really began to take shape. Because I was focused on another aspect of the design, I did not think about scale. Nor did I see that I was missing an opportunity to create a much more interesting quilt if I continued for a few more rows. If I then realized my design needed another row (or two) to allow the design to flow better, I became ambivalent: I wanted to be finished with the quilt, and yet I knew in my heart that the quilt wasn't visually completed.

Maybe you have had the same feeling about your own quilts. The quick fix is to ignore the problem; but then you may never be quite satisfied with your quilt. It is best to let the design dictate its needs. If this happens to you, and you want to increase your quilt's visual beauty, change your plans and continue the design. If your heart isn't in the quilt any longer, learn from the lesson, so you will not end up with the same results next time.

If your heart is still with the quilt, attempt to create a design that puts its best foot forward. Try not to jeopardize the design's potential simply because you are in a hurry to finish. Follow through with the flow of the overall design. Don't let much time pass before you continue. It's important to stay with your thought process and adrenalin flow. If you must take a break, write notes about your ideas so you don't forget them.

THE GOLDEN MEAN— ELEGANCE IN PROPORTION

Determining the size of your wall art is often a dilemma. Most often the relationship between the width and the length of an artwork is decided simply by happenstance or guesswork. Sometimes an artist attempts to be logical and decides to make her piece in a 1:2 or 3:4 ratio. In a 1:2 ratio, the shorter side is half the size of the other side (e.g. 3 feet by 6 feet) (Figure 5-7). This ratio is not particularly pleasing to the eye, even though it is often chosen. In a 3:4 ratio, the artwork's size may be 3 feet by 4 feet, or 6 feet by 8 feet, or any other size that conforms to that ratio (Figure 5-8). This causes some distraction because of its close visual similarity to a square. It does not allow much movement within the design.

Rather than the above-mentioned options, consider using the most-renowned system available for determining your wall quilt's width and length ratio. The most beautiful proportional formula is closely associated with nature and architecture. It was used in ancient times by the Greeks. It is called the *Golden Mean* or the *Golden Section*. A more subtle ratio than any other proportional system, the Golden Mean emphasizes elegance and beauty of line (Figure 5-9).

Figure 5-7. The 1:2 ratio is quite common in artwork. Generally, it does not result in the most pleasing design presentation.

Figure 5-8. The 3:4 ratio does not have quite enough length to present most designs to their best advantage.

Figure 5-9. The Golden Mean has an 8:13 ratio. Because of its beautiful proportions, it is widely used in art.

The ancient Greeks believed mathematics was an intricate part of the universe and of all natural and man-made design. Aristotle and the Greek mathematician Euclid were great proponents of this system for determining ratio. Both believed mathematics was a governing force in the universe.

Probably the most familiar example of the Golden Mean's ratio is the Parthenon, the chief temple of the goddess Athena. This temple was built on the Acropolis at Athens around 447 B.C. To this day it is considered one of the most beautiful examples of classical architecture. Although we are designing quilts, not buildings, we can use the same subtle ratio to create our own wall art. When we do so, we know its ratio will be visually successful.

The Golden Mean Ratio

The ratio of the Golden Mean is approximately 8:13 (8 parts to 13 parts). Using this ratio, a picture that is 8 feet wide will be 13 feet long. For our use, this ratio can be converted to 1:1.625 (13 divided by 8 = 1.625). This ratio is slightly more than a 2:3 ratio.

If you know how wide you want your art to be, multiply this proposed width by 1.625. The product will be the most appropriate proportional length for your picture's width. If you want your art to be 36" wide, multiply 36 x 1.625 to find the length. In this example, the length would be 58½".

(continued on page 66)

IF YOU WANT THE WIDTH TO BE:		THEN THE LENGTH SHOULD BE:		IF YOU WANT THE LENGTH TO BE:		THEN THE WIDTH SHOULD BE:	
12"	(30cm)	19½"	(48.75cm)	18"	(45cm)	11 1/16"	(27.69cm)
18"	(45cm)	29¼"	(73.12cm)	20"	(50cm)	12 5/16"	(30.76cm)
20"	(50cm)	32½"	(81.25cm)	24"	(60cm)	14¾"	(36.92cm)
24"	(60cm)	39"	(97.50cm)	30"	(75cm)	18½"	(46.15cm)
30"	(75cm)	48¾"	(121.87cm)	36"	(90cm)	22⅛"	(55.38cm)
36"	(90cm)	58½"	(146.25cm)	40"	(100cm)	24⅝"	(61.53cm)
40"	(100cm)	65"	(162.50cm)	42"	(110cm)	25⅞"	(67.69cm)
42"	(110cm)	68¼"	(178.75cm)	45"	(115cm)	27 11/16"	(70.76cm)
45"	(115cm)	73⅛"	(186.87cm)	48"	(120cm)	29½"	(73.84cm)
48"	(120cm)	78"	(195.00cm)	50"	(125cm)	30¾"	(76.92cm)
50"	(125cm)	81¼"	(203.12cm)	54"	(140cm)	33¼"	(86.15cm)
54"	(140cm)	87¾"	(227.50cm)	60"	(150cm)	36 15/16"	(92.30cm)
60"	(150cm)	97½"	(243.75cm)	66"	(175cm)	40⅝"	(107.69cm)
66"	(175cm)	107¼"	(284.37cm)	72"	(180cm)	44 5/16"	(110.76cm)
72"	(180cm)	117"	(292.50cm)	78"	(200cm)	48"	(123.07cm)
78"	(200cm)	126¾"	(325.00cm)	84"	(215cm)	51¾"	(132.30cm)
84"	(215cm)	136½"	(349.37cm)	90"	(225cm)	55⅜"	(138.46cm)
				96"	(230cm)	59 1/16"	(141.53cm)
				102"	(250cm)	62¾"	(153.84cm)
				108"	(275cm)	66½"	(169.23cm)
				120"	(300cm)	73⅞"	(184.61cm)

CONVERSION NOTES: *The numbers used for each system in the chart are not equivalent.*
To change inches to centimeters or centimeters to inches, do one of the following:

1. To convert inches to centimeters, multiply the number of inches by 2.54. Thus, 6" x 2.54 = 15.24 centimeters; 12" x 2.54 = 30.48 centimeters (nearly 30.50cm).

2. To convert centimeters into inches, divide the number of centimeters by 2.54. Therefore, 90 centimeters divided by 2.54 = 35.43" (nearly 35½").

If, however, you were certain of your artwork's length, and you needed to know the most appropriate width, divide the proposed length by 1.625 to obtain the most proportional width. For example, if you wanted your quilt to be 48" long, divide 1.625 into 48. The quotient is 29½". Thus, a quilt with a length of 48" would have a width of approximately 29½".

For your convenience, a *Golden Mean* ratio table with many possible wall art sizes is given on the previous page. If you want to use this highly regarded proportional system

and you know either the width or length measurement, use this table to obtain the second measurement.

Both the U.S. customary units (inches) and the metric system are included. The metric system is listed in brackets. The numbers used for each system are *not* equivalents, as that did not seem relevant. If you want to find a measurement's equivalent, see the conversion note below the chart. Inches have been rounded to the nearest usable fraction within our common ruler system (¹⁄16, ¹⁄8, ¹⁄4, ¹⁄2). Feel free to round off to the nearest inch or centimeter.

ACTIVITIES AND EXTENDED LEARNING:

1. Analyze your previously made quilt to check proportion and scale. Notice if your shapes are in good proportion to one another. Also check to see if you increased the sizes of any shapes in your quilt's border. If you did, note how it affected the quilt's overall visual unity. Do the border and overall design compete for your attention? If they do, consider how you might have created a successful border that did not affect the proportion negatively.

2. With your next wall quilt, decide to use the *Golden Mean* ratio. Figure the quilt's overall size; then determine the block size needed. Most likely you will need to draft your own pattern. If you have not drafted patterns before, or if you need a review, see Appendix II (page 120) in *The Magical Effects of Color* (see Sources).

3. If you want to experiment with proportion, consider changing the sizes of shapes within your quilt. This must be done carefully to be visually successful. It also may call for intricate drafting. Read Chapter Six for ideas on how to move the viewer's eye to your focus while keeping visual unity within your design.

4. If you want to experiment with scale, consider making a quilt using a large-scale format. To begin, it may be easier to work with realistic pictures. Take a close-up slide or snapshot of an object that particularly interests you. Use one portion of the picture to use as an exaggerated design focus. Georgia O'Keeffe's major work utilizes scale exaggeration. If you are interested in pursuing this design style, study her work. Check your local library or book store for her numerous art books.

51. RAPUNZEL, 1994, 8' X 5'
Daniele Todaro, Los Angeles, California
The children's fairy tale *Rapunzel* captured Daniele's imagination with its imagery of a lonely girl locked in a tower. Reds, greens, and gold are employed in this design, creating intense graphic imagery. Repetition of line, shape, and color brings harmony and unity to the design. Photo: Courtesy of the artist

52. SWIM IN THE FISHBOWL PLANET EARTH, 1991, 56" X 49"
Anna Edwards, Danville, California
Anna's design was inspired by the symbiotic relationship between man, animal, and nature she felt while in the South Pacific. As a result, Shakespeare's words, "one touch of nature makes the whole world kin" is the vision Anna attempts to achieve. Unity is created through color and shape repetition in the water. The foreground features create contrast and variation of shapes and colors. Photo: Ken Wagner

53. RIPPLING WAVES, 64" X 64"
Nobuko Kubota, Tachikawa-shi, Tokyo, Japan
This subtle quilt was inspired by a view of the coral island Hateruma from an airplane window. Nobuko used the Mariner's Compass as the center focus, representing a ship amidst rippling waves. The center focus beautifully contrasts the repetitious rippling wave effect. Photo: Courtesy of the artist

54. AMISH AMETHYST, 1986, 46" X 53"
Lois Embree Arnold, Chandler, Arizona
Amish Amethyst uses value gradations to help achieve unity. By gradually working from light to dark, Lois has created vibration in color. Photo: Louis Dickerson, Arizona

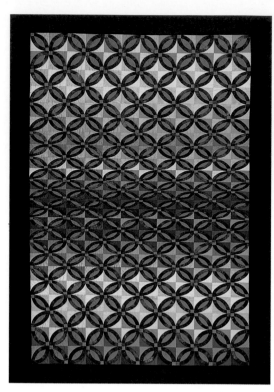

55. SANDIA WAVE, 86" X 63"
Yoshiko Ishikura, Gumma, Japan
Sandia Wave beautifully illustrates pattern, repetition, rhythm, and harmony. The subtle changing of the shapes' sizes and colors creates variation. Direction and movement are created through gradation. Photo: Courtesy of the artist

56. DILLY DAHLIA, 1993, 62" X 62"
Vicki Hurst, Redmond, Washington
Dilly Dahlia is an eye-catching quilt that uses a powerful pattern to achieve unity. Its wide selection of fabrics and color changes adds variation. Photo: Ken Wagner

57. Herb Garden, 89" x 89"
Nobuko Kubota, Tachikawa-shi, Tokyo, Japan
This stunning quilt was created using the Olympia and Star Flower block patterns. Through color and value changes, a three-dimensional effect of light and shadow results. The pattern has repetition, harmony, and unity, while the color changes give contrast and variation. Hand-pieced and hand-quilted. Photo: Carina Woolrich

Creating the Visual Dance

VISUAL BEAUTY— MORE THAN SKIN DEEP

When we first begin quilting, we are in awe of everything to do with quilts. We blissfully see all quilts as beautiful, and we imagine our closets will be filled with quilts in the near future. As we gain experience, reality sets in. We realize we are lucky to get quilts on every bed in our homes, let alone extra ones for closets. We also come to realize that not every block creates a beautiful design, and not every quilt is successful, let alone spectacular.

We begin to comprehend that there is more to quilting than simply learning techniques. Visual beauty of design becomes more important to us. As we become more discerning in our tastes, we see how small changes can make a quilt more visually pleasing: Perhaps the block used for the last quilt would have been much better if the large center shape or the corner shapes were broken into smaller pieces. Or maybe the setting could have been arranged differently to give better balance. Then perhaps we no longer want to make a quilt with 60 identical blocks—or even just 30. Or maybe we have been unhappy because our quilts have lacked *pizzazz*—or even beauty—and we need to rethink what we are doing. As we become comfortable with our technical skills, our interest in design should broaden. As experienced beginners, we should not only increase our technical skills, but also work toward strengthening our design skills.

This chapter, then, focuses on guidelines and ideas for bringing all the design elements together into a blend of visual beauty. I hope it will pique your interest, bring you new insights, and further stimulate your creative mind.

FAMILY RULES IN THE VISUAL ARTS— DESIGN PRINCIPLES

It is easy to understand design principles if you think of them as parts of a family. In a real family, each person has his own unique personality and talents. Beyond that, each individual is counted on to do specific tasks and work for the betterment of the entire family. The family works best and is most successful when each member works within the guidelines set forth. If anyone becomes out of control or demands total attention, the family unit suffers. Then the family cannot function to its best advantage.

Visual art works in the same manner. Each element is a member of the design family. Each has its own specific personality traits and visual talents. All elements have their own tasks to attend to within the design. Visual order must be present to achieve a harmonic relationship within the design. In art, this interaction between the various elements is guided by a broad group of concepts. These loosely developed parameters are brought together as the *principles of design.*

If a design is visually successful, everything works together to make a unified visual statement. However, if viewers focus on only one element within the design, the parts of the design are not working together. For instance, if people are only aware of quilting stitches in a quilt and the pieced or appliquéd design goes unnoticed, the elements are not working together as a visual family. Either the strength of the texture (the quilting) has overpowered the design because of its quantity, or there is weakness somewhere in the other design elements. Both conditions are detrimental to a design's beauty. Make certain, then, that you know and use the basics of design to increase the beauty and interest of your quilt.

Design principles are the building blocks you use to form your own unique artistic vision. These composition rules are structural guidelines to help you create wonderful quilts; they are not meant to restrict your creativity. Since beautiful technique cannot compensate for unfortunate design, the best incentive for using these principles is knowing you will achieve visual success with each quilt you create.

Good design is brought together through the unique blending of the design elements: line, direction, shape, color, value, proportion, scale, and texture. When these elements are beautifully or interestingly arranged, intuitive or conscious thought has guided them by making intelligent choices about design repetition, harmony, rhythm, gradation, unity, variation, contrast, dominance, balance, and focus.

To enhance your awareness of the design principles, take walks through your garden, or your neighbor's garden, or a park, or around a city block. Observe the many ways nature uses pattern, repetition, harmony, unity, variation, contrast, gradation, balance, rhythm, movement, and focus. Through these continual observations and your own experiments with their application, you will begin to find your own sense of design composition.

Figure 6-1. A seashell contains several repetitive design elements: line, shape, color, and texture. This repetition leads to rhythm and harmony. At least one element gives contrast to enhance beauty and interest.

The Importance of Unity

Every successful work of art, no matter the medium or style, must contain unity. Unity brings control or stability to the design. We need to see some sort of visual organization or relationship between the elements in the art. This association is not provided through a verbal or conceptual theme; it is purely visual. Quilts shown in this chapter all have unity. The quiltmakers have achieved it in a variety of ways.

When art has no unity, it appears confused, jumbled, and disconnected. It leaves us uneasy and uncomfortable. There is nothing that holds the work together visually. Everything looks haphazard. Fortunately, there are several easy ways to achieve unity, so this should not be a problem in our work.

Lack of unity is one of the biggest reasons most sampler quilts are visually unsuccessful. It is also a significant problem for quilters and other artists who are just beginning to create abstract or contemporary designs.

ACHIEVING UNITY THROUGH REPETITION, RHYTHM, AND HARMONY

Unity is primarily achieved through repetition, rhythm, and harmony. Color, value, shape, direction, texture, and line are all elements that may be repeated throughout the design. When elements in a design are repeated, a pattern develops. See Photos 5, 18, 25, 51, 61, 70, 78, and 137.

Pattern is powerful. It can be hypnotic, like waves lapping on the shore, or soothing, like grasses blowing slowly in the wind. It can even be suggestive, like the aurora borealis as it moves across the sky in flowing rhythm (Photo 3), or subtle, like the stones we walk along every day. Pattern promotes a sense of rhythm (Photos 28, 34, 49, 53, 55, 57, 60, and 79). In turn, this rhythm creates visual harmony; harmony between the elements brings about a sense of unity.

UNITY WITH VARIATION AND CONTRAST

Because pattern is caused by repeating one or more elements, it gives us a sense of order. Unfortunately, repeating every element creates monotony. So besides repetition, you must also allow for variation or contrast.

Variety enhances the design, as it adds interest to the repetitive nature of unity; it provides contrast amid sameness or predictability. Variety in a design can range from a dramatically eye-catching focus to subtlety. It can be created through color, value, shape, line, direction, or textural change. Both unity and variety should be present in any design, because these two principles are inseparable. When one is not present, the design suffers visually.

It is important to remember that a design's highlight is rarely found in the repetitious pattern; instead, our eyes are most interested in the area that visually interrupts the pattern—where contrast or variation exists. Thus, breaking up a pattern becomes paramount to a design's strength (Photos 24, 50, 55, 78, 84, and 124).

NATURE'S USE OF UNITY AND VARIETY

Nature showers us with many examples of unity and variety. A seashell contains several repetitive design elements (line, shape, color, texture), but subtle contrasts are present (Figure 6-1). Flowers also illustrate the concept of unity combined with variety and contrast. Observe various flowers in your garden to see how cleverly unity and variety are partnered. A pansy would be nondescript without its contrasting inner face (Figure 6-2). A beautiful tulip shows unity in its form, but its subtle color variation is the element that causes us to catch our breath in wonder (Figure 2-10). A quilt's success is much the same as nature—variety and unity increase the design's success; this, in turn, adds to our appreciation of the quilt.

Figure 6-2. Nature uses unity, variety, and contrast to create beautiful designs. A pansy would be nondescript without its contrasting inner face; its face adds interest. Photo by the author

Quilts worthy of our admiration include subtly beautiful quilts *Four Seasons* (Photo 79), *Roudo Veueziano* (Photo 19), the dramatic *Fire Facettes With Two Parrots* (Photo 58), *Stravinsky's Rite* (Photo 78), and other lovely quilts such as *Celtic Peony Rose* (Photo 11) and *Herb Garden* (Photo 57). These quilts all have a sense of rhythm, harmony, and unity. Yoshiko Ishikura's lovely *Sandia Wave* (Photo 55) also shows wonderful repetition, pattern, rhythm, and harmony. The subtle changing of the shapes' sizes adds the necessary interest and variation.

Rapunzel (Photo 51) by Daniele Todaro is another great example of a successful artwork in which many elements work toward unity. Daniele allows repetition of line, shape, and color to present visual control, yet she uses enough variation to maintain excitement and interest throughout. It is a design that compels us to return to look at it again—and again. While browsing through this book, notice the many quilts that contain wonderful examples of successful unity combined with variation and contrast.

Designs Lacking Variety

Too much unity usually results in bland and uninspiring art. Overly unified art lacks interest because it displays no variety or contrast. It does not require us to give it more than a passing glance, since there is nothing further to investigate or wonder about. Thus, achieving unity through repetition, rhythm, and harmony can be much like walking a balance beam. There may be only a fine line between too much harmony and not enough. This fine line is one of the challenges we encounter as we create. It sets our adrenalin flowing, allowing our excitement, apprehension, and exhilaration to come forth.

When you create new designs, another means to achieve unity is by putting shapes close to one another. Shapes in close proximity to each other appear to have a relationship. In contrast, when shapes are isolated, it is very difficult to show that a bond exists between them (Figures 6-3 and 6-4). When your design includes isolated shapes or patterns, find some other means to create an association, so that they appear unified.

Figure 6-3. When shapes are isolated, no bond exists. You must then find some other means to create an association so they appear unified.

Figure 6-4. Shapes in close proximity appear to have a relationship. Their visual bond promotes unity.

Unity is often established in nature through a bridge of gradation. For instance, the two seasons of winter and summer are extreme in many areas. To go immediately from the coldest part of the year to the hottest would be too great a shock to our systems. So nature provides us with a graduated bridge between the two extremes. These graduated climatic changes are spring and autumn. They move us gently from one extreme to another.

Art can work in the same way. A bridging gradation of shapes, sizes, colors, or values can be used to soften differences or extremes, while it promotes unity. *Herb Garden* (Photo 57) is a lovely quilt using gradation of color and value to create its design contrast. This results in a quilt with an added dimension of depth and outstanding visual beauty.

Amish Amethyst (Photo 54) also uses value gradations to help achieve unity. If the lightest and darkest colors were placed side by side, the visual effect would be quite different. By gradually working from light to dark, the artist has attained a quilt that vibrates. Wendy Richardson has also combined color and value gradations to create her subtly beautiful *Saturday Morning* (Photo 73).

Direction and Movement Through Gradation

Bridging gradation allows for extremes in the design without shocking the viewer. It often brings a sense of direction to the design. For instance, changing the sizes of shapes from one part of the design to another can be done by forming a visual bridge between the largest and smallest shapes. Yoshiko Ishikura does this beautifully with *Sandia Wave* (Photo 55).

Because the bridging effect carries our eyes along with it, we feel a sense of movement. This visual bridging can be done either very subtly or with a pronounced effect, depending on the artist's desire. *Sandia Wave* creates wonderful direction and movement through gradation.

THE PRINCIPLE OF VISUAL BALANCE— THE STRONG, SILENT PARTNER

If a design is balanced, we are unaware of this principle's existence in the work. If balance does not exist in an artwork, we become very aware of it, as the lack of visual balance makes us uncomfortable.

In art, balance is attained through distribution of visual weight. Visually speaking, large shapes weigh more than small shapes of the same color. Light-colored shapes weigh less than dark shapes of the same size. So when you put

shapes of many different colors together in a design, it creates a visual balancing act.

Balance and Gravity

Generally, we want to see more weight at the bottom of our art rather than in the middle or at its top. This visual reaction to weight relates to our innate knowledge of gravity; we expect heavy objects to fall to the ground. So placing our heaviest colors, values, and objects at the bottom of our designs gives us a sense of well-being or of being grounded.

There may be times when you choose to place the heaviest weight elsewhere in your design, however. When doing so, you must compensate for this placement by balancing it with visual weight elsewhere in the design. Be certain your design is balanced, even if it doesn't conform to the laws of gravity (Figure 6-5).

Figure 6-5. We expect the heaviest objects, or the heaviest part of an object, to be near the bottom of a design. This gives us a sense of well-being (pine cone on right). If the heaviest object or the heaviest part of an object is placed elsewhere in the design (pine cone on left), this must be compensated for in order to achieve visual balance.

Conversely, we expect the lightest colors to be somewhere in the top half of the design, seemingly reaching upward to the sky. When we see what we naturally expect, we feel a sense of comfort or calmness. Thus, if you create the unexpected (*i.e.*, a light object near the bottom edge), take special care to compensate for this surprise. The design must still be balanced. It is much more challenging to achieve visual balance when you choose to stretch our visual expectations.

Visual weight can be changed by manipulating color and value scales, by working with intensity changes, and by varying the sizes of shapes. High-valued colors (light), bright colors, and spaciousness are considered light in weight. Low-valued colors (dark) and shapes that appear solid, contained, or muted in color look heavy.

Types of Balance

Three types of balance are used in art: symmetrical, asymmetrical, and radial. Each type of balance has its own characteristics and sense of design style. Two are fairly easy to achieve, while the other is most challenging. Figures 6-6 through 6-9 demonstrate the visual differences between the different types of balance.

SYMMETRICAL BALANCE

Symmetrical balance is the easiest to work with. One half of the design is a mirror image of the other half (Figure 6-6). Traditional quilts based on symmetrical balance include those in Photos 104, 123 and 129.

Figure 6-7. Assymmetrical balance is achieved through distribution of visual weight. Placing the tree in the center of this picture creates visual distress because the design is unbalanced. All of the interest is on the right side; nothing catches our eye on the left side.

The graceful lines of federal buildings, historic churches, and elegant estates are based on symmetry. This kind of balance is also called bilateral symmetry. Animals, including man, are considered bilaterally symmetrical. Symmetrical balance is most preferred and used by beginning quilters and design students. It is not complicated, so visual success is fairly certain.

Symmetry and Art

Symmetrical balance is the most formal of the three types of balance. Often very ornate drawings and decorative art are created in symmetry. Many needlework patterns are based on this form of balance. Scandinavian and Northern European decorative art is created in symmetry. Even South and Central American folk art shows numerous examples of symmetrical balance.

Most traditional quilt block patterns are symmetrical. As beginners, this allows us to use patterns that give us ample opportunity for success. If we choose our fabrics and colors carefully, we can be fairly assured that mirror-image symmetry will work for us. Symmetrical balance also can help quiet an overly busy surface design.

The greatest visual disadvantage of symmetrical balance is the possibility of being too repetitive, static, and unexciting. Care must be taken, then, to include some variety or contrast in our symmetrical designs.

Figure 6-6. Symmetrical balance is the easiest type of balance to work with. The pine tree exhibits symmetry in nature because the sides appear identical.

Figure 6-8. By placing the tree farther to the left, asymmetrical balance is achieved. The strength of the lower trunk balances with the tree's windswept features on the upper right. As a result, our eyes move from the left to the right, sensing balance.

Figure 6-9. Asymmetrical balance can be achieved by manipulating shapes, sizes, colors, values, and textures. By strategically placing other objects near the tree, asymmetrical balance has been achieved.

ASYMMETRICAL BALANCE

Asymmetrical balance is achieved through distribution of visual weight. It has a more informal appearance than symmetry. Although it seems incidentally arranged, it can be complicated to create an excellent asymmetrical design (Figures 6-7 and 6-8). Asymmetrical balance is difficult to achieve because both sides of the design surface must either weigh the same visually or they must be equally interesting, even though they are not similar. Both the visual weight and the eye-catching attraction are created through manipulating colors, shapes, sizes, values, and textures (Figure 6-9).

Like other forms of balance, asymmetrical design is found in nature. A spider web is one of the most beautiful examples of asymmetrical design in nature. Japanese gardens are marvelous examples of asymmetrical design. Ikebana, Japanese flower arranging, utilizes asymmetrical design in nature by showing careful regard for form, harmony, and balance, as it relates to nature.

The Teeter-Totter Effect

Asymmetry is best described as a *teeter-totter effect*. As young children, remember how we had to shift our bodies forward or backward to distribute the weight evenly before we could teeter-totter? The heavier person moved closer to the center, while the lighter one moved outward. If our weights were similar, both of us positioned ourselves equal distances from the teeter-totter's center (Figure 6-10).

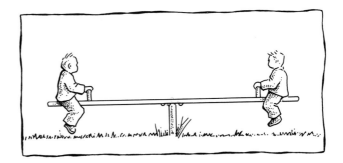

Figure 6-10. Visual balance is similar to playing on a teeter-totter. When both sides are of equal strength, balance is achieved. Here, the children are similar in size and weight so they are well-balanced. Visual balance works similarly.

When we teeter-tottered with a parent, we had two choices to teeter-totter successfully: Two or more of us had to sit together on one side to balance the adult's weight. If we didn't do this, we could remain in the air indefinitely—with no hope of returning to the ground without help (Figure 6-11); sometimes balance could be achieved if the adult moved close to the center point as we moved out to the edge of the board on the opposite side (Figure 6-12).

Figure 6-11. An adult and a child on a teeter-totter present a weight problem. The adult is much too heavy for the child's weight. Imbalance occurs so the play is unsuccessful. Visual balance reacts the same way: A large object usually overwhelms a small object, causing visual imbalance.

Figure 6-12. If the adult and child reposition themselves on the teeter-totter, they can succeed in their play. To do this, the adult moves toward the center, while the child moves farther away from the center. In asymmetrical design, a large object can also be moved closer to the center while the smaller one moves away from it. This change subtly shifts the visual weight, resulting in balance.

Balancing the Scales

In high school physics classes, we relearned our earlier lesson with a balance scale. Two items of unequal weight can be balanced on a scale just by repositioning the items. To do this, we had to bring the heavier object closer to the center of the scale, while moving the lighter object closer to the edge of the scale, depending on the disparity between the weights.

Figure 6-13. If the child invites his friends to join him on the teeter-totter, then together they can successfully teeter-totter with the adult. Their combined weight will be similar to the adult's. This compensation can also be used to achieve visual balance in asymmetrical design. Several small objects may be used to balance the weight of a large object.

Balancing Visual Weight

Visual balance is identical in concept to the teeter-totter and the balance scale. In order to achieve balance between a visually heavy shape and a lighter one, the objects must be distributed in a similar fashion. Visual weight management must be done with care, as the larger shape should not be too close to the middle of the design, and the smaller one should not go too far into the edge of the design surface.

It may be necessary to place several smaller shapes on the opposite side from a large shape to help distribute the visual weight (Figure 6-13). The spacing between these smaller shapes is done instinctively. There is no one right way; there will be several possible options. After experimenting, place them in the position that most pleases you.

Achieving Asymmetrical Balance Through Contrast

Color and value play a very important role in asymmetrical design. We are able to manage the visual weight more easily if we can manipulate colors and values. Contrasts of pure and toned hues, light and dark values, warm and cool colors, blurred and distinct patterns, textured and smooth surfaces all help distribute weight between objects. For instance, our eyes are more attracted to color than to a non-colored object. Thus, a small colored shape can visually weigh as much as a large gray shape (Figure 6-14). A large shape of high value (light color) will weigh less than one of low value (dark color) (Figure 6-15).

Figure 6-14. Contrasts in color can help achieve asymmetrical balance. A small colored shape can visually weight as much as a large gray shape.

Figure 6-15. A large shape of high value (light) will weigh less than a large shape of low value (dark).

Our eyes are more interested in complex objects than in smooth, non-textured shapes. Consequently, we can also distribute visual weight by drawing the eye's attention to both sides of the design. A big shape automatically catches our eye. So we can place an intricately created small shape on the other side. Its complexity will demand our attention. This intricacy adds weight to the object, thereby compensating for its lack of size (Figure 6-16).

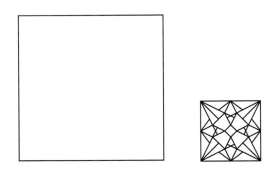

Figure 6-16.
A big shape naturally catches our eye. Its visual weight can be balanced by a smaller, more intricate shape. The latter's complexity will compensate for its lack of size.

It is important not to put all your visual strength in the largest shape in your design. For example, if you have a large shape in your design that is both intricately made and brightly colored, you would have to work hard to create equal visual weight on the other side of the design surface. Most likely you would have to add many other shapes to compensate for the attention drawn to the large, intricately-pieced, dramatically-colored shape. Ignoring this would create an extremely unbalanced design.

Sometimes you can achieve balance between two extreme objects through gradation. The progression of change causes the eyes to move along the design, from one area to another in a smooth fashion. Accents placed diagonally at opposite intersections can also help achieve balance within a design.

You will find numerous examples of asymmetrical balance in this text. They vary in style, subject matter, coloration, and technique. Take the time to study these quilts; you should also enjoy their wide individual differences. Some quilts using asymmetrical balance include Photo 1 on page 9 and Photos 10, 26, 27, 32, 40, 51, 52, 58, 62, 64, and 71.

Taking the Plunge—
Creating an Asymmetrical Design

Before working on your asymmetrical design, make written notes of your ideas. (Naturally, some of these concepts will change during the design process.) Ask yourself several pertinent questions: What will your dominant color family, scale, and value key be? What shapes will you primarily work with? Will your design show direction? How will you attain unity? How will you provide variety? Will you create a focal point? If so, how?

Do not expect to know everything about your design before you begin. However, having an initial direction to follow is helpful. You can make as many changes as you wish. Your end result may look nothing like the design you expected to create.

When working with asymmetrical design, it is easiest to work on a design wall. This can simply be a flannel sheet temporarily pinned to your wall. This working space allows you to stand back from the design to observe its progress. If you have difficulty getting far enough away from your design to see its strengths and weaknesses, use a reducing glass. This is a glass that reduces objects rather than magnifies them. It is shaped similarly to a magnifying glass, and it can be bought from a photography store.

Begin working where you feel most comfortable in your design. This could be in the middle, a bottom corner, a top edge, or any other place in your design. Attempt to work intuitively as much as possible. Allow time for your design to simmer in your mind; don't rush your progress. Give yourself time to see your design when you are not actively working on it. Often when you look at it casually, new ideas pop into your head or needed changes become more apparent.

Radial balance moves a design outward from the center. Radial designs are often circular, although some merely imply circular energy. The central focal point is established automatically because of its radial nature (Photos 54 and 103). Radial balance is prominent in nature. Dahlias, camellias, daisies, roses, and sunflowers are just a few of the many flowers that exhibit radial balance (Figure 4-1). A stone tossed in a pond gives a rippling effect, illustrating radial balance. The sun itself represents radial balance.

Traditional quilt patterns with obvious radial balance include the Mariner's Compass (Photos 53 and 76) and the Giant Dahlia (variation, Photo 56). Quilts that imply radial balance are Log Cabin Barn-Raising (Photo 70) and Trip Around the World (Photo 93). Radial balance is usually exciting to work with because it can be so dynamic. It represents explosive power with its seemingly limitless energy.

Radial balance often brings us some of the most beautiful designs. Additionally, these designs are relatively easy to make into successful quilts, because they exude natural balance. *Midnight Sun* (Photo 119) is a wonderful design exhibiting radial balance. Another beautiful example of radial balance is Lorraine Simmon's floral appliqué, *Shalimar Garden* (Photo 88).

DOMINANCE

A beautifully successful design exhibits the principle of dominance in all of its design elements. One color family is given the dominant role within the design; likewise, one value key is used predominantly; one shape will also dominate. In other words, one member of each design element visually represents its entire element. Most of these choices are made intuitively. We are not even aware we are making such subtle decisions.

Competition between two parts of an element results in visual distraction. This can happen before we are aware of it. For instance, yellow doesn't need much urging before it visually overtakes the strength of all other colors. If a color inadvertently becomes too pronounced, lessen its frequency or make it less intense (tone it down).

FOCUS OR EMPHASIS

Beautiful art generally has an area of emphasis within the design. This point of interest is often created through contrast. For instance, if you are working primarily in the tone scale, you may create a focal interest by placing more intense colors in the area you wish the viewer's eyes to be drawn to (Photos 13, 18, and 46). Or, if your design is predominantly created in the rich, dark low key, you can lead the eye to a particular area of your design by placing lighter-valued shapes where you want emphasis (Photo 54).

Contrasting shapes is another easy way to draw our eyes to focus on a certain area of a design. If you added a circle to a work of art that was made primarily from squares, our eyes would automatically focus on the circular shape. The vertically straight lines set against the diagonal background in *Challenge With Red* (Photo 18) catch our attention. The organic birds contrasting with a picture made entirely with triangles create the focus in *When East Meets West* (Photo 15).

Movement or graduated change can also draw the eye along a certain path. Whenever your design shows a directional emphasis, the eye will move to the end point. This directional line may be created through continuous movement of one shape, color, or value. At other times, the arrangement of elements may imply movement. The eye enjoys suggested movement, so this kind of focus can be extremely successful (Photos 55, 71, and 78).

Positioning Your Point of Focus

It is as important to position your focal point correctly as it is to determine what will be focused. Generally, it is considered too predictable and elementary to locate the focal point exactly at the center of the design; most areas of interest are placed elsewhere. There are times, however, when it is appropriate or best to place your focus in the center. Certainly, radial balance naturally emphasizes a central focus; a sun setting on the water may also be especially becoming when it is vertically centered.

A simple means of determining the focal point place-ment is the photographer's *rule of thirds* (Figure 6-17). Simply divide your design surface into thirds, both verti-cally and horizontally. Place your focal point on or near one of the four areas of intersection. Although this is a great tool, do not feel you must rigidly adhere to this guideline.

Another method of determining a focal point is by placing it in the design where the distance between the focal point's center and each of the four outside edges is different (Figure 6-18). This gives you more latitude than the *rule of thirds*.

Mistakenly Diluting the Strength of Your Focal Point

Don't accidentally dilute the strength of your intended focal point by distracting the eye with another area of interest. For example, if you decide to focus on an area in the upper left corner of your design, don't place a strong-ly contrasted shape somewhere else. This causes competi-tion between the two and dilutes your design's strength. Generally, competition between design elements occurs when you use an overabundance of contrast.

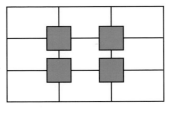

Figure 6-17. Photographers use the *rule of thirds* to choose their focal placement by dividing a picture into thirds, horizontally and verti-cally. The focal point lies within one of the intersecting areas.

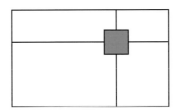

Figure 6-18. You may determine a focus area by finding a point where the distance between the focal point's center and each of the four outside edges is different.

ACTIVITIES AND EXTENDED LEARNING:

Activity I:
Learning About Your Individual Tastes

You can learn a lot about your own design styles by analyzing quilts you most love and least like. Often you learn more from studying the latter. The more time you can work on this exercise, the more revealing it will be for you. This activity should be divided into three separate sessions, so your responses and decisions are fresh. Use several quilt publications for this activity.

SESSION 1:
With paper and pencil, draw columns with the following six headings: (A) I am ecstatic about the quilt! (B) I like the quilt very much. (C) The quilt is OK. (D) I have no reaction toward the quilt. (E) I don't like the quilt very much. (F) I intensely dislike the quilt!

Go through the publications, observing each quilt printed in color. Without analyzing, place each quilt's name, publication, and page number in the column that reflects your immediate reaction. Continue doing this until you have placed at least eight to ten quilts in each column. The more quilts you list, the better you will be able to discover your design style.

SESSION 2:
Review your chart. First, study all the quilts you listed as absolutely loving (column A). On another paper, write down everything about each quilt that pleased you. After you have done this for each quilt, notice if there are any reoccurring features. Summarize (in writing) what features you most positively respond to in these quilts.

Now study the quilts you most intensely dislike (column F). Write down everything about each quilt that visually distracts you. After you have completed the list, notice if certain characteristics repeat themselves. Summarize your findings.

Next, go to all the quilts you listed in column C—those quilts you had no strong feelings toward or against. Analyze these quilts. List what you notice about each of them. What parts of each of these quilts are similar? If you have time and interest, do the same type of analysis and summarization for the remaining columns.

SESSION 3:
Reread your summaries. They should be insightful. From this information, attempt to draw a conclusion as to the types of quilts your intuitive self likes best. What design characteristics are you most drawn to? Which ones should you avoid? This activity should accurately determine the style of quilts you should spend your time creating, as well as those you should not. Focus on creating quilts you are most drawn to.

Activity 2:
Playing with Unity

A. PROXIMITY
Draw two identical rectangular shapes 6" x 10". In one, glue five different shapes far away from each other. In the other, place another set of five shapes close to each other. Place the two rectangles on a wall; stand back at least 10 feet. Notice which one pleases you more. Which one seems more unified?

B. REPETITION AND DIRECTION
Draw three rectangles 6" by 10". Choose your favorite shape to work with (i.e., circle, square, triangle, rectangle). Make several of these shapes in different sizes, colors and values (fabric or paper). Create three different designs by using these following methods of placement: 1) overlapping the shapes; 2) grouping the shapes; and 3) moving the shapes across the design surface. After each arrangement is done to your satisfaction, place the rectangular design on the wall. Have you been able to create unity through direction and/or repetition successfully? If not, make changes now.

C. UNITY AND VARIETY
Make a rectangle 6" by 10". Cut out several objects of the same shape, size, color, and value. Arrange them in a design. Make another rectangle of the same size. Cut the same number of objects, but this time vary their shape, size, color, and value. Arrange them in a design. Put both rectangles on a wall. Observe which design is more pleasing. Which was easier to create an interesting design with?

D. STRETCHING YOURSELF
Determine your design interests and loves. Grant yourself permission to create quilts that excite you. Then give yourself permission to purchase the materials you need to create these images. Allow yourself time and space to work. Realize you are the only one who can make the difference between wishing to create a quilt and doing so.

An Exhibition of Spectacular Quilts

58. FEUERFACETTEN MIT 2 PAPAGEIEN (FIRE FACETTES WITH TWO PARROTS), 1990, 193CM X 193CM (76" X 76")
Erika Odemer, Munchen (Munich), Germany
Erika's exquisite color sense is exhibited in this stunning quilt. Using the traditional Log Cabin technique as her inspiration, Erika has created a fascinating design by using a wide variety of shapes and sizes for the block centers.
Photo: Patricia Partl, Munchen, Germany

59. FANS AND FEATHERS, 1993, 85" x 103"

Sonja Palmer, Plymouth, Minnesota

This quilt was inspired by a pattern in the September 1982 *Quilter's Newsletter Magazine*. Using this pattern as a base, Sonja incorporated her own appliqué design and border. Fan and Nosegay blocks were used for the basic design elements. Using her own dyed fabric, Sonja created a lustrous effect with blue value changes. Her quilting design added beautiful texture to the design. Photo: Ken Wagner

60. EARTH'S ELEMENTS
1994, 52" x 48"
*Doreen Thompson,
Richland, Washington*
Through Doreen's use of
color, fabric selection, and
block manipulation, the
traditional pattern Quilt
Box has evolved into an
exciting contemporary
design. Photo: Ken Wagner

61. TAIPEI, 1993, 42" x 42"
Judy Sogn, Seattle, Washington
The computer game *Taipei* and a painting were the
dual inspirations for Judy when creating this dynamic
quilt. *Taipei* vibrates with stunning color. Photo:
Dennis Sogn, Seattle, Washington

62. THE OTHER SIDE OF MY
GRANDMOTHER'S FLOWER GARDEN,
1993, 64" x 75"
Jane Kakaley, Bellevue, Washington
Jane has created a joyful quilt that flows
with happiness. Her color use and
design application are wonderful. She
has embellished her design with hand-
dyed and hand-painted fabric. The
pattern for this quilt is available from
Jane (see Sources). Photo: Ken Wagner

63. CHROMA III: VINIFERA, 1993, 52" x 52"
Jane Hall, Raleigh, North Carolina
A master technician of the Pineapple Log Cabin, Jane has been doing
a series of colorwash quilts using this design. *Chroma III: Vinifera* is a
lovely Pineapple design created in the harmonic analogous color
scheme. Jane has incorporated the appliqué border beautifully to fit
with the body of the quilt. The quilting enhances the overall design.
Jane works on a removable paper foundation for stability and precision
(see Sources). Photo: Ken Wagner

64. SPLIT RAIL, 1994, 25" x 40"
Cynthia England, Houston, Texas
Split Rail is a charming quilt depicting the quiet life in the country.
By capturing the setting's mood, Cynthia treats us to another
delightful pieced-picture quilt. She worked from a photograph to
create her design. By carefully looking, you may see the cat hidden
in the quilt. (See Sources regarding Cynthia's pieced-picture
patterns.) Photo: Ken Wagner

65. ANOTHER TIME'S FORGOTTEN
SPACE, 1993, 103" X 69"
Gail Biddle, Mill Valley, California
This stunning quilt is an adaptation
of a 1970s poster promoting a rock
concert. Simple block strip-piecing
was used throughout the quilt's background. Hundreds of fabrics were
used to achieve subtle gradation from
light to dark. Feathers were first
curve-strip-pieced and then snipped
apart on their lower edges for a
three-dimensional effect. They were
then heavily layered and hand-
appliquéd. Photo: Tom Yarish,
California

67. TRANSITION, 1993, 28" in diameter
Donna Warnement, Houston, Texas
Donna created this challenge quilt with
the traditional block St. Lawrence
Seaway. Starting with an 8" square in
the center, she pieced 21 blocks into
her quilt. Nineteen different fabrics
helped Donna achieve the design's
striking effect. Photo: Ken Wagner

66. PATHWAYS, 1993, 54" X 54"
Alison Goss, Cumming, Iowa
Pathways, like Alison's other recent creations,
evolved from internalized visions of landscapes—pictures she carries in her head and
heart, which often begin during her summer
hikes in both mountains and deserts. Finding
endless sources of inspiration in nature,
Alison continues to create wonderful quilts
that celebrate the beauty of nature. Photo:
Courtesy of the artist

68. MIDNIGHT ADVENTURE, 1994, 67" x 84"
Donna Schneider, Kelowna, British Columbia, Canada
This quilt began as a take-off of a Log Cabin Barn Raising set, with each block having a light and dark side. As Donna's adventure with 14 fabrics grew to more than 200, her design began to develop its own personality. Her fabric use helped create movement in the surface design. *Midnight Adventure* was inspired by Margaret Miller's book *Strips That Sizzle* (see Sources). Photo: Ken Wagner

69. FOREST FLOWING, 1992, 138" x 76"
Karen Perrine, Tacoma, Washington
A breathtaking work of art, *Forest Flowing* is part of Karen's forest landscape series. It is composed of a simple arrangement of rectangles and large triangles, cut from intensely patterned and colored hand-painted fabric. Karen has purposely used a close-up view to draw us into the scene, so that our imaginations may begin to blend with the visual stimulation of this exciting piece. Machine-pieced; hand-appliquéd; machine-quilted with Sulky metallic thread. Photo: Mark Frey, Tacoma, Washington

70. SUMMER DAWN, 1994, 86" x 86"
Kaye Rhodes, Annandale, Virginia
Summer Dawn, vibrating with color, is a spectacular Log Cabin Barn Raising quilt. Kaye's major focus was color selection and fabric placement. The result is a breathtaking visual treat. The 144 Log Cabin blocks were machine-pieced on temporary foundations. Kaye drafted the block in its off-center configuration. Then she carefully traced the drafting 18 times. With seven layers of paper beneath each tracing, she needle-punched each stack, thus marking her foundations before sewing. Kaye likes foundation piecing because of its accurate results. Photo: Lloyd Wolf, Arlington, Virginia

71. DON'T GO GENTLE, 1993, 53" x 60"
Charlotte Warr Andersen
Salt Lake City, Utah
This beautifully poignant quilt was
inspired by a photo of Charlotte's
father, taken 25 years earlier. She began
this quilt as her father's health began to
fail in late 1992. It is a most moving
quilt, as Charlotte has captured the
essence of her father's spirit as he walks
in comfortable solitude with nature.
Don't Go Gentle is a pieced-pictorial
quilt, created with wools, silks,
polyesters, and cottons. Photo:
Borge Andersen & Associates, Utah

72. REVELATION, 1990, 48" x 52"
Judy White, Ellington, Connecticut
This beautifully innovative contemporary
quilt began as a traditional block. Judy
started by creating a star on a cube.
Then she manipulated the design until
it formed a pattern she liked. Judy's
intuitive fabric choices are wonderful.
By careful study, you can see that many
fabrics create surprising interactions with
their neighboring fabrics. This pieced
design is embellished with bugle beads,
seed beads, and antique jet beads. Photo:
Ken Wagner

73. SATURDAY MORNING, 1992, 66" x 80"
Wendy Richardson, Brooklyn Park, Minnesota
The subtle beauty of Wendy's quilt is breathtaking. Although it appears she has used hand-dyed
fabrics, she has magnificently blended subtle prints and drapery fabrics to achieve her flowing color
effect. The design began with the traditional Barbara Frietchie Star, but as Wendy worked, her
intuitive design sense began making changes. Photo: Dan Kahler, Minnesota

74. MOUNTAIN SUNRISE, 1993, 68" x 78"
Susan Duffield
Sidney, British Columbia, Canada
This stunning Thousand Pyramid design was
not put together by chance fabric placement.
Instead, Susan arranged the shapes to give the
feeling of mountain and sky. The border,
inspired by Charlotte McFarland, was created
as an extension of the inner design. Hand-
and machine-pieced; hand-quilted. Photo:
Gary McKinstry, Victoria, B.C., Canada

75. DEVELOPMENT, 1993, 120CM X 90CM
Rosemarie Guttler, Kuppenheim, Germany
Rosemarie has a magical way with fabric, color, and
design. Her curved, organic designs are soft, subtle, and
calming. Her designs beautifully exhibit the elements
and principles of design. Photo: Courtesy of the artist

76. COMPASS ROSE, 1988, 88" x 100"

Joy Baaklini, Austin, Texas

Created by a contemporary quiltmaker, this stunning Mariner's Compass is a magnificent heirloom quilt that accentuates the successful blend of texture, subtle color use, and traditional design. Joy has used the border and quilting design to reiterate the theme of the sea. In the open space, intricate stitching incorporates dolphins and seahorses swimming around the compass. The border creates a wave that is the background for a traditional cable design. The body of the quilt is machine-pieced and hand-quilted; the border is hand-pieced, hand-appliquéd, and hand-quilted. Photo: Ken Wagner

77. WINCHESTER CHARM, 1989, 99" x 106"
Marie Goyette Fritz, San Diego, California
This fantastic Tumbling Block quilt is a two-sided charm quilt. Marie has used 2,829 different fabrics to hand piece
this design. Many of these fabrics include 1930s and 1940s designer fabrics from Paramount Studios. The Winchester
Mystery House in San Jose, California, was under continual construction during its owner's lifetime. Since Marie plans
to add three blocks every year to this quilt, she has named it after the house. The quilt will eventually belong to
Marie's daughter who was seriously ill while the quilt was being made. Photo: Courtesy of the artist

78. STRAVINSKY'S RITE, 1985, 76" X 60"
Alison Goss, Cumming, Iowa
Inspired by Stravinsky's music, *The Rite of Spring*, Alison has created a fantastic display of design that excites us with its color movement. Alison, the quiltmaker who introduced the concept of transposing bargello needlepoint designs to quiltmaking, creates wonderful quilts that are richly woven with spectacular color play. Photo: Sharon Risedorph, California

79. THE FOUR SEASONS, 1991; EACH OF FOUR PIECES 12" X 12"
Deirdre Amsden, London, England
Deirdre is a master at blending fabrics and colors together to create wonderful illusions. Using primarily toned fabrics, Deirdre creates *The Four Seasons*, a beautiful design that represents sunshine and showers. Private collection. Machine-pieced and hand-quilted. Deirdre is the author of the book *Colourwash Quilts* (see Sources). Photo: Courtesy of the artist

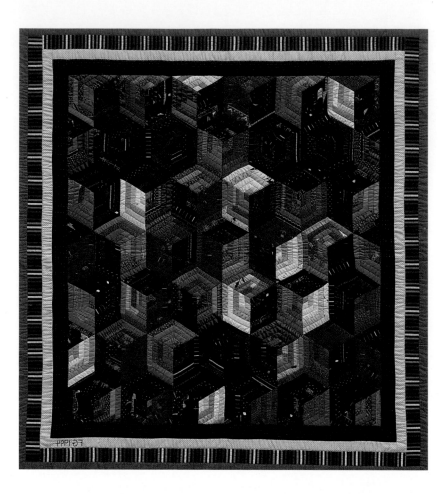

80. RIO STREETDANCE, 1994, 68" x 64"
Flavin Glover, Auburn, Alabama
Rio Streetdance is a spirited, innovative Log Cabin quilt. Using the hexagon Tumbling Block pattern as her inspiration, Flavin created her Tumbling Block design by joining three diamond Log Cabin blocks. The warm colors appear to advance, while the cool colors recede. Photo: Ken Wagner

81. SPUMONI SUNSET
1994, 51" x 81"
Caroline Perisho, Bainbridge Island, Washington
This refreshing quilt has included a touch of whimsical fantasy to realism. Caroline attempted to capture each member of her family after a fabulous day at the beach. Hand-appliquéd and strip-pieced. Photo: Ken Wagner

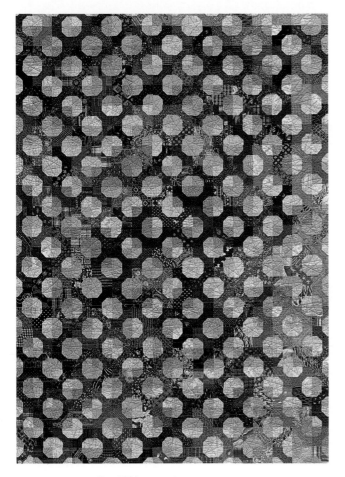

83. BLACKFORD'S BEAUTY, 1994, 72" x 82"
Lauralee Hanson, Bremerton, Washington
This traditional four-patch pattern has additional interest because Lauralee has made each block different in its color and fabric application. Photo: Ken Wagner

82. DANIEL'S BOW TIE, 1992, 72" x 92"
Maureen H. McGee, Lansing, Kansas
Maureen created this design by drifting the colors across the quilt's surface. Maureen prefers to have a definite color plan when creating scrap quilts. She particularly likes the colors to flow into each other. To construct, Maureen used the method described in Judy Hopkin's book *Fit To Be Tied*. Photo: Ken Wagner

84. SEPTEMBER MOUNTAIN, 1986, 56" x 68"
Carol Ann Wadley, Temple, Texas
Using the traditional pattern Maple Leaf, Carol Ann has created a fantastic autumn quilt. This innovative quilt was created while Carol Ann lived in Oregon. She used Mt. Hood, Oregonians' favored mountain, as a backdrop in her quilt. Collection of Alice Greene. Photo: Bill Bachhuber, Portland, Oregon

85. LIVING STREAM, 1990, 50" x 45"
Ruth Laine Bennett, Paoli, Pennsylvania
This original design was inspired by nature's beautiful landscapes and the writings in Rachel Carson's *Silent Spring*. Wanting to live in harmony with nature, Ruth has created this quilt to celebrate the initiative and courage taken by individuals who have worked hard to give us back our living streams. Three-dimensional trees, lace foam, metallic rocks, and hand-painted sky combine to add realism to this scene. Photo: Ken Wagner

86. NORTHERN REFLECTION, 1991, 57" x 46"
Ruth Laine Bennett, Paoli, Pennsylvania
A cruise to Alaska inspired talented Ruth Bennett to create this lovely landscape quilt. She has used calicoes, other commercial fabrics, tulles, metallics, synthetics, and dyed fabrics. Ruth appliqués and quilts simultaneously. She calls this technique appliquilting. She has embellished her scene with three-dimensional trees; the reflection was created by using an overlay of three different tulles. Photo: Ken Wagner

87. SUNRISE, SUNSET, 1993, 54" x 42""
Ruth Laine Bennett, Paoli, Pennsylvania
This southern scene has been beautifully enhanced by Ruth's glorious hand-painted sky and water fabric. Ruth has used her own innovative techniques to create her fantastic design. Three-dimensional work, trapunto, and overlays all work to bring realism to this scene. Photo: Ken Wagner

88. SHALIMAR GARDEN, 1991, 90" x 90"
Lorraine Simmons, Graham, Washington
This exceptionally gorgeous medallion quilt is Lorraine Simmons' interpretation of the historic *Paradise Garden* quilt created by Rose Kretsinger in the 1930s. This pattern and its variations were originally made in the mid-1800s. It was known then as *The Garden*. Lorraine drafted the pattern from the cover photo of *American Patchwork Quilt*, published by Spencer Museum of Art, The University of Kansas. Lorraine's quilt is created entirely by hand. All feathers are stuffed. Photo: Ken Wagner

89. SHALIMAR GARDEN, 1991, DETAIL
Lorraine Simmons, Graham, Washington
Lorraine is noted throughout the Pacific Northwest as a master of appliqué technique. Her exquisite handwork is breathtaking. This detail allows you a closer view of her work. Photo: Ken Wagner

90. HORIZON, 1993, 64" x 90"
Junko Sawada, Kanagawa-ku,
Yokohama-shi, Japan
Junko's creative desire is to bring something new and refreshing to old traditional
patterns. She does this beautifully in all
her quilts. Here, Junko has achieved her
goal by creating this delicate and refreshing design by using a modified Log Cabin
technique. The movement of the air and
wind is expressed by a group of colored ribbons. The ribbons dancing in the sky are
reflected on the water. Photo: Courtesy of
the artist

92. JADE BAY, 1992, 85" x 95"
(shown on the facing page)
Donna Pringle, Oliver, British Columbia, Canada
This breathtaking quilt, created by Donna,
is an impressionistic picture of beautiful Lake
Kalamalka in British Columbia. Donna has
created this scene by combining strip piecing,
appliqué, and Seminole piecing. The quilting
greatly enhances the design, accenting depth
and movement. Private collection. Photo:
Ken Wagner

91. WHAT THE WINDS SAW, 1992, 82" x 72"
Junko Sawada, Kanagawa-ku,
Yokohama-shi, Japan
This beautifully innovative Log Cabin quilt
creates the impression of birds joyfully
 riding the wind currents on a blustery day.
Although a few birds are quite apparent,
some are subtly flying far into the distance.
This is another marvelous quilt made by
Junko Sawada, a truly talented quilt artist.
Photo: Courtesy of the artist

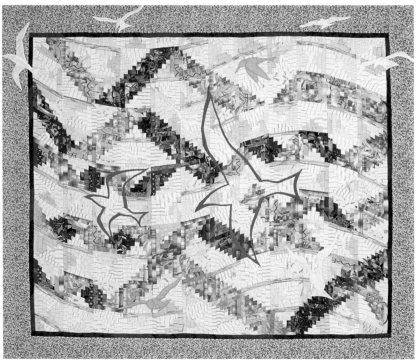

$\int$ECTION TWO

Designing Spectacular Quilts

Section Two is dedicated to our medium's premier concern—how to create a spectacular quilt through superb use of design, fabric selection, and textural quilting. Because we use fabric and the textural quilting line as a painter would paint and brush, special attention must be given to our medium. To make spectacular quilts, not only must we be able to envision and design what we want to create, but also we must be clever enough to have selected and bought the fabrics for our creative endeavor. Then, we must know how to use these fabrics to their fullest potential. Additionally, we must have the ability to enhance the design with the textural qualities of the quilting line. Because it is important that we nurture our interest in creating spectacular quilts, a wealth of design, fabric, and quilting information is offered in Section Two for your consideration.

93. TRIPPING AROUND THE WORLD IN A SPLASH OF COLOR, 1992, 86" x 96"
Joen Wolfrom, Fox Island, Washington
This Trip Around the World quilt was made with nearly 10,000 postage-stamp size squares for
Danielle Wolfrom to celebrate her college graduation. Through fabric and color blendings, the
illusions of luminosity, iridescence, opalescence, and luster were created. This quilt was one of three
stolen in January 1993 in an airline baggage robbery in Miami, Florida. Photo: Ken Wagner

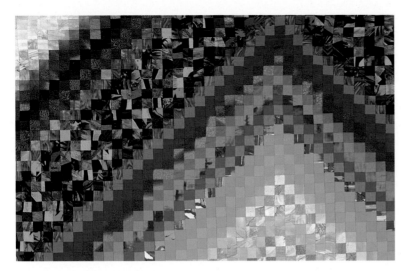

94. TRIPPING AROUND THE WORLD IN A SPLASH OF COLOR, 1992, DETAIL
Joen Wolfrom, Fox Island, Washington
A wide variety of fabrics were used in this quilt, ranging from subtle to dramatic, and from strongly toned to vibrant. The design of each fabric was allowed to fall naturally within the quilt's pattern. Photo: Ken Wagner

95. MELLOW MORN IN THE FOREST, 1987, DETAIL
Joen Wolfrom, Fox Island, Washington
A close inspection shows some of the subtle color selections used in this off-set Log Cabin quilt. The texture of the quilting line enhances the design rather than reiterating it. Photo: Ken Wagner

96. MELLOW MORN IN THE FOREST, 1987, 118" x 112"
Joen Wolfrom, Fox Island, Washington
This offset Log Cabin quilt was inspired by Maria McCormick-Snyder's early work. The delicate coloration was used in the split-complementary color scheme of this king-size bed quilt. There are no two blocks using identical fabric placement. Photo: Ken Wagner

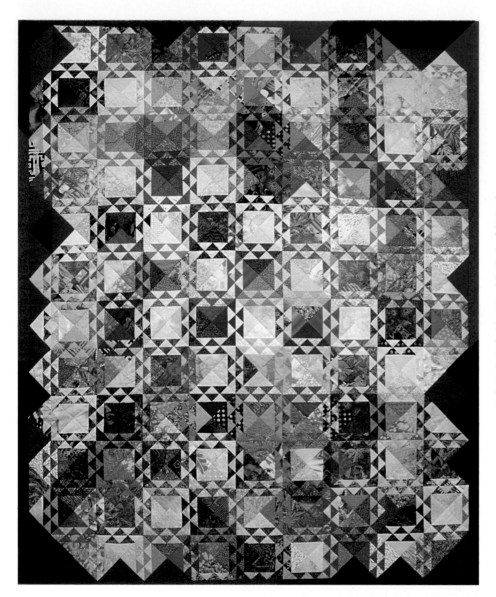

97. TRANSFORMATIONS, 1992, 85" X 104"
Barbara E. Friedman and Lorane Feinberg,
San Diego, California
The traditional pattern North Wind was
used to create this outstandingly beautiful quilt. The fabric and color choices
create vibrancy and excitement.
Transformations was an opportunity quilt
made to support the San Diego Head
Injury Program. Lorane, an artist and
head injury survivor, helped with the
color and design effects. The blocks
were made with random color combinations. While designing on the wall,
Barbara made specific blocks to fill
empty block spaces. Private collection.
Photo: Carina Woolrich, California

98. TRANSFORMATIONS, 1992, DETAIL
Barbara E. Friedman and Lorane Feinberg,
San Diego, California
This detail allows us to see some of the
fabrics used to create this beautiful quilt.
Photo: Carina Woolrich, California

99. COLOURWASH WINDMILLS, 1994, 25½" x 25½"
Deirdre Amsden, London, England
In this quilt, Deirdre, one of the leading colorists in our field, has used color, value, and intriguing fabrics in a fascinating manner to create a design that appears to float above the quilt's surface. *Colourwash Windmills* is in The Quilters' Guild 90s Collection. Photo: Courtesy of the artist

100. SHIMMERING TRIANGLES
NORTH WIND, 1986,
67" x 79"
Sharyn Squier Craig, El Cajon, California
This shimmering design was created using the traditional block North Wind. An antique quilt in the *1984 Quilt Engagement Calendar* was Sharyn's inspiration. She has used toned fabrics with accents of warm shades to enhance the vibrating movement. Machine-quilted by Shirley Greenhoe. Photo: Ken Jacque, California

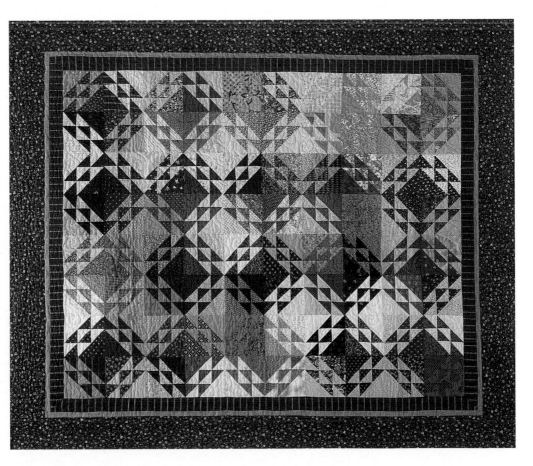

The Quilter's Palette—Fabrics

In the quilt world we use fabric similarly to the way a painter works with her palette of paints. If we make wise fabric choices, we can create incredible effects with our designs. Often the difference between a mundane quilt and one of extraordinary beauty or interest is simply the difference in fabric selection and use.

Barbara Friedman's and Lorane Feinberg's *Transformations* quilt (Photo 97), based on the North Wind pattern, is an example of an extraordinarily beautiful and interesting traditional quilt. Their selection and placement of fabrics has made this an exceptional quilt. The quilt fascinates us with its shimmering effect. A detailed view of one small section gives you an idea of the fabrics selected and their placement (Photo 98).

Buying and selecting fabrics is a personal affair. For a quiltmaker, it is an extremely important step in the creative process. With our traditional buying habits, however, the visual success of our quilts has much to do with the fabrics available in our color choices on the particular day we visit the fabric store. This method of selecting a quilt's fabric leaves a lot to chance. By selecting our project's fabrics in a very short time span (sometimes with only one shopping trip), we significantly limit our potential fabric creative play.

Additionally, while we are working on our in-progress quilts, lovely fabrics regularly appear in the stores—and disappear. But because we are focused on our current projects, we tend not to see or purchase these other fabrics. We rarely give ourselves the luxury of buying fabrics for which we have no plans. Sadly, hundreds of fabrics come and go between our current and future projects, and we miss chances to add great fabrics to our collections.

One of the long-term effects of buying in the traditional manner is that we never establish a really thorough fabric collection. Instead, our collection is spotty, and often comprised primarily of leftover fabrics from past projects. It would be far better to broaden our buying habits by continually adding fabrics to our collections, which increases our color, value, and textural options.

Because I was disappointed by fabric choices when I shopped for my quilt projects, and because I knew it was unreasonable to expect any fabric store to have an unlimited array of fabrics, I determined I needed to change the way I bought fabrics for my quilts. While my frustration increased with my inability to find the fabrics I needed to create the images in my mind, I also found it difficult to maintain my interest when I made a quilt with 20, 30, 60, 120, or 144 identical blocks. These two dilemmas led me to change both my fabric-buying habits and the way I selected and used fabrics in my quilts.

In this chapter, I would like to share these ideas with you. Additionally, I have included information about hard-to-find fabrics and those that are difficult to use successfully in many of our quilt designs. I hope my past experiences and current methods will give you incentive to rethink buying, selecting, and using fabrics.

New Ways To Buy and Select Fabrics for Quilts

I no longer buy fabric for a particular quilt project. Instead, whenever I visit a quilt store I buy whatever fabrics please me on that day. Sometimes I find myself buying wild, strong fabrics; on another day, I may purchase only autumnal fabrics; perhaps on another trip I find my fabric stack filled with subtle, toned fabrics. I do not analyze my choices when selecting fabrics. I purchase what I am visually drawn to—without justifying the reason. Sometimes only a few fabrics pique my interest; on other days I find myself with a glorious pile. Rarely, however, does this method of buying affect my budget, as it's a gradual acquisition.

When selecting fabrics, I never concern myself with how I will use the fabric. I am simply provisioning a fabric cache for future projects. In any given year, I find my selection varies in style, scale, color, design, and texture.

I am particularly fond of working with painterly fabrics. These include large-print florals, hand-dyed fabrics, and decorator fabrics. I also buy many fabrics for their back-side textures and colors. Most back sides of fabrics are toned, so you increase your muted fabric collection just by considering their use. They are especially good for creating atmospheric perspective and enhancing subtlety.

I almost always buy one-third yard of each fabric. If I am exceptionally excited about a particular piece, I may purchase one-half yard. If the fabric is a large print that has wonderful color blends (e.g., huge flowers), I buy one design repeat. Most large-pattern repeats are between one-half and seven-eighths yard or meter.

I do not concern myself about buying enough of one particular fabric for any given quilt, since I am no longer interested in making a quilt with just a handful of fabrics. I am extremely interested in having a wide selection of fabric. For me, buying one-third yard pieces of three different fabrics is much more appealing and exciting than buying one yard of one fabric. I no longer worry about running out of any fabric while working on a quilt. Since I use an enormous variety of fabric in a given project, if I run out of one fabric, it is hardly noticeable. Incredibly, there always seems to be another to take its place.

Although I have worked in this manner since the early 1980s with solid-colored fabrics, it has only been since the late 1980s that I have bought print fabrics this way. Even though I have far less quantity of fabrics in my collection than most quiltmakers, I have acquired a wonderful array. It's exciting to buy fabrics not knowing what you will be using them for—but knowing they will be a very welcome selection sometime in the future.

To help illustrate how I work with fabric, two quilts and a collection of blocks from two other quilt projects have been included as examples of these concepts of selecting and using fabrics.

TRIPPING AROUND THE WORLD
IN A SPLASH OF COLOR
98" x 82"

In *Tripping Around the World in a Splash of Color* (Photo 93), the traditional fabric placement was cast aside. I wanted the colors, patterns, and textures to blend and flow spontaneously from one to the other. Therefore, I opted to use 1" squares (finished) rather than the more traditional 2" squares. With few exceptions (primarily the central area), the fabrics I used were prints.

The center area yellows, yellow-greens and greens were from a packet of Carol Esch's hand-dyed tints, which I bought specifically for this quilt. The remainder of the fabrics were pulled from my shelves. They were part of my eclectic fabric collection of one-third to one-half yard pieces—all accumulated from past fabric-store wanderings. In this quilt, I used approximately 90 different fabrics.

The clear yellows, yellow-greens, greens, soft powdered blues, and lavenders were chosen for the center colors to promote the illusion of luminosity. As I began to work on the quilt, new ideas began appearing in my mind. Soon I could see luster, opalescence, and iridescence evolve, as fabrics seemed to call for me to include them.

Using print fabrics caused interesting things to happen from square to square. Sometimes strong value or color changes appeared. At first I was concerned about these happenstances. In the end, I decided to let the fabric designs fall naturally within each square without any interference from me. I quickly found their incidental interactions were far more exciting than anything I could have planned (Photo 94, detail). I was sad when I put my final fabric in place, because I still had more fabrics I wanted to include in the quilt.

MELLOW MORN IN THE FOREST
118" x 112"

In the Log Cabin quilt *Mellow Morn in the Forest* (Photo 96), no two blocks use the same identical fabrics, although there are more than 100 blocks. I pulled together every cream, apricot, peach, pink, coral, grayed green, and grayed blue-green fabric that I owned. I cut strips (1" and 1½" wide) from all the fabrics. I hung the strips on a wooden clothes rack next to my sewing machine. Each time I began a new block, I would randomly pick its fabrics. It was fun choosing the fabrics for each block, and I could hardly wait to see how the block looked when it was finished (Photo 95, detail). In addition, it was exciting arranging the blocks because their hues interacted so interestingly. There were so many ways the blocks could have been put together; it was hard to make a final choice.

 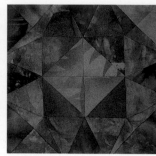  

Figure 7-1   Figure 7-2   Figure 7-3   Figure 7-4

Figures 7-1 to 7-4. *Curved Jewels* sample blocks, 1983, 12", *Joen Wolfrom, Fox Island, Washington.*
Each block of *Curved Jewels* was created with its own fabric selection. The background was created from differing value and hue variations of gray. The foreground design was created primarily in hues of blue, plum, rose, pink, and purple. Accents were in yellow and orange. The fabrics in each block's center square were selected first. Then the remaining block fabrics were chosen. Later, these blocks were made as part of Joen's continual hand rehabilitation after being bitten by a dog in 1992. Pattern ©1983 Joen Wolfrom. Photo by the author

CURVED JEWELS
84" x 60"

In 1983, I designed the block Curved Jewels, but I didn't create a quilt from this design until the early 1990s. More than one hundred fabrics were included. Some I only used once; others I used several times. The fabrics were a combination of hand-dyed and off-the-bolt fabrics. For the latter, I used fabrics that gave beautiful color blends, rather than calicoes or fabrics with strongly pronounced patterns.

I decided to make the quilt's background cool gray. So I pulled out all the grays in my fabric collection that appeared on the cool side. I ended up using about 20 different gray fabrics. Some were blued, some charcoal, some pinkish, some quite neutral. They included many different values and textural effects. I placed them randomly in the blocks promoting shadows and light.

For the foreground pattern, I decided to use a wide variety of colors and values. I began each block by choosing the center fabrics. From there, I chose fabrics for the jewel points, using three to eight fabrics for these points. After these were chosen, I selected fabrics for the rest of the block (Figures 7-1 to 7-4). Because the fabrics were not placed in any set order within the block, it allowed for wonderful design play when the blocks were put together. Sometimes it was difficult to put only one strong fabric in a block because it looked out of place in its block setting. However, when the blocks were put together, these colors reacted beautifully with the rest of the blocks.

DUTCH ROSE IN THE SUNSET
IN-PROGRESS QUILT

I am in the process of making a Dutch Rose quilt. Again, I have made no special trip to the fabric store to buy fabrics. I am using my eclectic collection of fabric to meet my needs. If I run out of a fabric while making this quilt, I am sad to see it go. However, I have found there is always another wonderful one waiting to take its place.

This quilt's background is planned as a sunset, beginning at the bottom with brilliant yellow, and moving upward into apricot, orange, coral, red, magenta, and violet (Figure 7-5). In the bottom blocks I have used about 20 different yellow fabrics for the sky. These range from soft creams to brilliant yellows and golds. The other sunset background fabrics will also include a wide variety of fabrics, which will create subtle changes in values and hues. I plan to have the Dutch Rose foreground pattern range from dark to middle-valued, vibrant colors at the bottom of the quilt (Figures 7-6 to 7-9) to softer yellows, apricots, and corals in the upper blocks.

I am having a great time putting these fabrics together. In any one block, I randomly include fabric triangles and squares, sometimes using 20 to 30 different fabrics. Once I have selected my fabrics, I arrange them on a piece of flannel pinned to my wall. Then I stand back to see how the fabrics interact with each other. At that time I make any needed visual adjustments.

Each block is really fun to create, because the different fabric combinations are transformed into unique blocks with their own colorful personalities. I look forward to beginning each block, and I can hardly wait to finish each one, so I can see what the end result will be. It is an energizing activity filled with great joy.

Putting the Quilt Blocks Together

I prefer to sew my quilt blocks together after all blocks have been constructed. I do this for several reasons. Since I am using dozens of fabrics, and each block is unique, the blocks need to be arranged for visual balance. If a strong fabric has been used in many blocks, these blocks need to be spread around to achieve unity throughout the quilt. Also, if a new, pronounced-pattern fabric is included in some of the later-constructed blocks, these, too, can be arranged throughout the design.

Usually when I complete each block, I put it on my flannel wall. I continue playing with the arrangement of the blocks as they are finished. I work in this manner until I have only a few blocks to finish.

It's difficult to get uniquely created blocks to work perfectly together. Therefore, when I have completed all but four or five blocks, I stop and begin arranging them into their final placement. This may take a few days to work out. A few blocks may not be visually pleasing anywhere. They are often my very first blocks. These I set aside.

Eventually, all of the workable blocks will be positioned on the wall in their final arrangement. Since I have not finished constructing all the blocks, and I may have a couple of discards, several *block holes* will be present throughout the quilt. These empty spaces are usually places where no existing block works well. So I design my last blocks specifically to fit in each of those holes. They are created to interact well with their neighboring blocks. In other words, my last four or five blocks are *custom-made* for their specific placements.

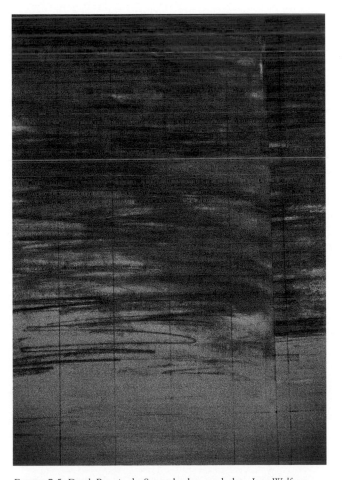

FIGURE 7-5. *Dutch Rose in the Sunset* background plan, *Joen Wolfrom, Fox Island, Washington* This rough color guide is the sunset plan for the background colors to be used in the quilt *Dutch Rose in the Sunset*. The quilt's actual background colors may vary somewhat from this color plan. Photo by the author

Figure 7-6

Figure 7-7

Figure 7-8

Figure 7-9

Figures 7-6 to 7-9. *Dutch Rose in the Sunset* sample blocks, 12", *Joen Wolfrom, Fox Island, Washington.*
These blocks are samples of those to be placed in the bottom of the quilt where the sunset is most intense. Notice there are many yellow fabrics of varying values and intensities used in each block. The center square fabrics were selected first. The fabrics for the star points and the dimensional ribbons were then chosen to enhance the inner star fabrics. Each block varies in the colors and fabrics used. Photo by the author

MAKING WISE CHOICES— STAYING AWAY FROM PROBLEM- PLAGUED FABRICS

Certain fabrics are consistently detrimental to the visual outcome of a quilt. Because so many really wonderful fabrics are available today, I find little reason to buy fabrics that present more problems and distractions than beauty. Naturally, there are times when these problem-plagued fabrics do come into their own glory, so knowing when to use them successfully is important.

Attempt to put fabrics together to make a specific statement. The fabrics should come together in unity to create your visual statement. If one fabric pulls out visually so that your eye is drawn to it *without artistic intent*, the fabric has either been placed incorrectly in the design or the fabric is completely wrong for the quilt. Either way, it spoils the total effect. Certain fabrics are noted for this and can be categorized as problem fabrics. They can be used, but when you include them, recognize their liabilities and work to make them an asset in your design. If this cannot happen, choose not to use them.

Fabrics With White Backgrounds or Pattern

Fabric with white incorporated can be difficult to use with other fabrics. There are exceptions. Because white pulls out visually, it can be an extremely distracting color. Our eyes will automatically be drawn to any white in a design. Thus, if this is not your intent, substitute an off-white or blush-white fabric (a very light tint) for white.

Combining white with tints is usually very successful because all tints are made from white. Additionally, certain theme quilts warrant using white: A valentine quilt needs red and white. Many people enjoy working with strongly contrasting colors. White is a perfect partner to use with brilliant, strong colors for high contrasts.

Strong Geometric Pattern

Some of my favorite calicoes of the 1980s never made it into a quilt because they would not blend easily with other fabrics. My eyes were drawn to them immediately, demanding my instant attention. This happens particularly with a strong geometric pattern that is rigidly positioned on the fabric. If it is small in size, it can often be used with no visual problems. However, if it is considered a medium- or large-scale print, it will probably be too strong to combine successfully into a unified statement.

Strong Linear Pattern

Sometimes a beautiful fabric surprisingly takes over visually because of its pronounced design. Marbled fabric is often too strong to blend readily with other fabrics. Liberty Fabrics have this visual problem. To diffuse this strength, these beautiful fabrics may be broken up into small pieces that evoke great beauty, while working together with other fabrics. Deirdre Amsden is a master at working with these fabrics to create beautiful works of art. One of her quilts is shown in Photo 99.

Multi-Colored Calicoes

The most beautiful calicoes use value and intensity changes of one or two hues to create their design. When the fabric includes three, four, five, or more color families, it tends to look busy. In a traditional quilt design, the fabric color least wanted will almost always call attention to itself. For this reason, be careful when using multi-colored calicoes. They are perfect for distant flowers, meadows, spectators, and other such uses.

If a fabric does not have a dominant hue, it tends to appear busy and blur into the neighboring fabric. When used unintentionally, these can diminish the quilt's attractiveness. However, if you want to make a scrap quilt or a colorwash quilt (Photos 14, 24, 133, and 136), these negative characteristics become positive, workable features. Deirdre Amsden uses these fabrics expertly to create amazing designs (Photo 99). By using small portions of each fabric, Deirdre creates beautiful color washes (Photo 79). As she works, she eliminates fabric design problems that would distract from the overall impression.

Strongly Contrasting Colors

Be careful when using calicoes that contain two very pronounced, strongly contrasting colors. For instance, if you intend to make a valentine Log Cabin quilt, red fabrics will be on one side and white fabrics on the opposite side. At first glance, any red-and-white floral fabric may seem perfect. When you begin making the Log Cabin blocks, the fabric with a contrasting red-and-white design will have too much red to be used in the white side, and it will have too much white for the red side. Thus, even though the fabric may incorporate the exact colors you need, using it will be visually detrimental.

When two colors compete with each other for visual dominance, your eyes will bounce back and forth from one color to the next, not knowing which to look at. These fabrics should be avoided at all costs. They have virtually no redeeming qualities.

Use Plaids, Checks, and Stripes With Care

Although plaids, checks, and stripes can be a wonderful addition to some designs, they are distracting when improperly placed. Only include them in your quilt when the design will be enhanced by their use. Try to use plaids, checks, and stripes that have a straight weave unless you prefer a homespun appearance. In most designs, it is disconcerting to see crooked plaids, checks, or stripes.

Allowing Yourself To Change Your Mind

Some fabrics appear to be perfect while on the bolt; however, when they are placed with other fabrics, they become the center of attention—they take away from the design's unity. If you cannot dilute the fabric design's strength, seriously consider eliminating that fabric from your quilt. If you are vacillating in your decision, go with your intuition. In the end, if a fabric looks great, keep it in; if the fabric bothers you visually in some way, take it out.

LOOKING FOR THE ELUSIVELY CLEAR FABRICS

Tints are clean and clear, and lighter than pure colors. Most light-colored fabrics are not tints, however, as they have a grayed cast. Manufacturers and dye artists who make tint fabrics start with a white material—pure white. Most commercial fabric starts as an off-white color. This subtly affects the fabric colors, resulting in a tonal effect. I buy tints whenever I find them. Tints are important for attaining illusions, so they are worth hunting for.

Pure colors and some shades are equally difficult to find for the same reason. They, too, are useful for wonderful illusions. Currently, many hand-dyed fabric artists start with bleached fabrics, so that they can create clean, clear, dynamic colors. We can hope that fabric manufacturers will increase their use of white fabric for a starting base, so we may have greater selections of fabrics using tints, pure hues, and shades.

INDIVIDUALISM AND FABRIC CHOICES

It is exciting to see the wonderful, individualistic ways people are putting fabrics together to make truly magnificent quilts and textile art. Our fabric choices allow for all types of moods, imageries, and suggestive ideas. Drama and subtlety, winter and summer, spring and fall, night and day—all are attainable through our fabric choices. Scores of quilts throughout this book illustrate beautiful fabric use very well. At your leisure, study the quilts in this book to see how fabrics have been brought together successfully in a design.

ACTIVITIES AND EXTENDED LEARNING:

1. Sizing Up Your Fabric Collection

This exercise will give you experience in discerning the difference between the four color scales in fabric. This is an important step in understanding color. Also, by doing this exercise, you will be aware of gaps in your fabric collection, as well as areas of overabundance. You will need one sheet of paper, a pencil, fabric scissors, glue stick, and your fabric collection.

REVIEWING AND CATEGORIZING THE COLOR GROUPS

Review the differences between pure colors, tints, warm shades, cool shades, and tones (see Chapter 4). Make certain you understand their different characteristics. Now draw seven rectangular shapes on a sheet of paper (*e.g.*, 2" x 3"). Each rectangle will represent one of the following groups of colors: 1) pure colors, 2) tints, 3) warm shades, 4) cool shades, 5) light-valued tones, 6) medium-valued tones, and 7) dark-valued tones.

DIVIDING YOUR FABRIC INTO COLOR-SCALE COLLAGES

With your fabric collection in front of you, stack your fabrics in seven piles, each representing one of the above divisions. (You don't need to use all of your fabric.) Once you have a good selection of fabrics together, begin cutting small pieces of fabric from each pile. Glue these pieces into the appropriate rectangle, making a fabric collage.

Place your fabric collages on a wall. Stand back to analyze your collages. If you find a fabric pulling out from the rest of a rectangle's fabrics, most likely the fabric has been misplaced. If fabrics are properly placed, the colors work well together. You may have some empty rectangles, because you do not own a particular color scale of fabric. In contrast, you may have an overabundance of one or two groups. Most people have more toned fabrics than any other kind. Tints and pure colors are usually the groups with the least amount of fabrics.

MAKING CHANGES IN YOUR FABRIC COLLECTION

If you find you are lacking in certain areas, attempt to resolve the problem by adding those color scales into your fabric collection. At first, it may seem uncomfortable to buy these fabrics, because you are not used to them. Also, if you have never used them, you may be unaware of their existence. By making the effort to introduce all groups into your fabric collection, you will have more ability to create spectacular quilts.

2. Assessing Problem-Plagued Fabrics

Analyze your fabric collection to see if you have any fabrics that are categorized as problem-plagued. Pull all of these fabrics out of your collection to analyze. Stack them in groups according to their design characteristics (*e.g.*, strong geometric design, strong value contrast, white in design, no dominant color, etc.) After grouping them, notice if you have a strong tendency toward buying one type of design. What do you think draws you to this fabric style? Can you work well with it? How can you use it to its best advantage? If you do not want to use this type of fabric design in the future, be careful on your fabric-buying trips. It is often difficult to break a long-standing habit. By choosing other fabrics, you are working out of your comfort zone. Since there are so many wonderful fabrics to choose from, this should not be a problem for long.

3. Assessing Past Work

If you have been displeased with any of your past work, analyze those projects to see if the problem lies in your fabric selection. The three major areas of concern, with regard to fabric, are usually color choices, value changes, and print design. Assess your work to see if any of these are problem areas in your quilts.

4. Building a Dynamic Fabric Collection

Begin selecting and buying fabric in the manner discussed in this chapter. When you visit a fabric store, buy fabrics that please your eye and make you feel good. If you shop regularly and buy during all seasons of the year, you should have a well-rounded fabric collection within a short period of time. By buying intuitively, your fabric choices will better reflect your inner self. Your color and design style will become more pronounced in your quilts.

There is no *right* amount of fabric to purchase. It depends on your storage capability and budget. For a general guide line, fat quarters and $1/4$-yard pieces are good amounts for picking up accent-colored fabrics. Buying $1/3$- to $1/2$-yard pieces and design repeats will allow you to acquire a wonderful array of fabric. Within a few years, you will have a great collection of fabrics—which will continue to grow and evolve.

5. Choosing Fabrics for Your Next Quilt Project

Plan your next quilt project. Rather than using only a few fabrics for the design, plan to use scores of fabrics, as described in this chapter. Be certain to use fabrics with similar coloration throughout the quilt to promote unity. However, give each block its own fabric personality for interest and variety. When nearing the end of your construction phase, remember to place your blocks on the wall. Make custom blocks where needed.

101. SETTING SUN
1983, 48" x 36"
Joen Wolfrom, Fox Island, Washington
Quilting lines were used to outline land elements and create details. Machine-pieced and hand-quilted. Photo: Ken Wagner

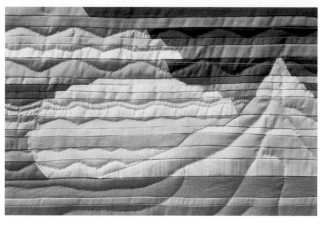

102. SETTING SUN, 1983, DETAIL.
Joen Wolfrom, Fox Island, Washington
When hand quilting, Joen matches the thread color to the underlying fabric. Therefore, the sun is quilted with yellow thread, the mountain in this detail with gray thread, and the sky with a wide variety of sky-colored threads to match the fabrics. Hand-quilted. Photo: Ken Wagner

103. REFLECTIONS ON THE SOUND, 1981, 30" x 30"
Joen Wolfrom, Fox Island, Washington
This offset Log Cabin design was created in a complementary color scheme. The textural design created through quilting radiates from the center, giving the illusion of lines moving outward. As the quilting line moves through the logs, the quilting thread changes color to match the under-lying fabric. Machine-pieced and hand-quilted. Photo: Ken Wagner

104. DIMENSIONS OF DAWN
1988, 37" x 37"
Shirley Perryman,
Cary, North Carolina
Using an analogous color scheme,
the Twelve Triangles pattern's
lustrous effect is achieved through
value changes in the narrow border
strip. This enhances unity through
repetition and harmony. The textural
effects of the intricate quilting design
have given the quilt additional interest and depth. Photo: Courtesy of
the artist

105. AGE OF AQUARIUS, 1990, 60" x 60"
Beth P. Gilbert, Buffalo Grove, Illinois
Inspired by Wucius Wong's *Principles of*
Two Dimensional Design, Beth has created
movement through color placement and
quilting lines. The background stippling
adds contrasting pattern to the design.
Photo: Courtesy of the artist

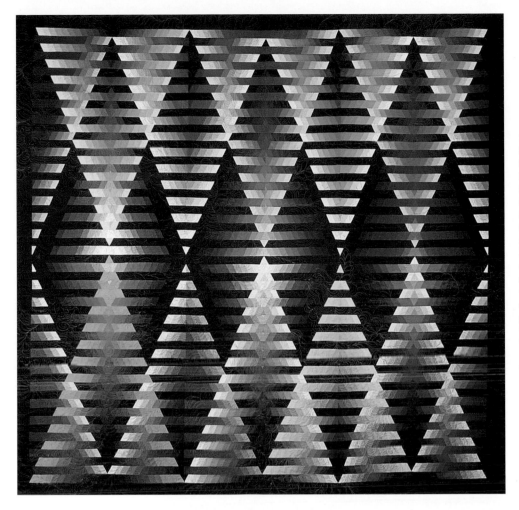

106. ILLUSION #2, 1993
89" x 88"
Caryl Bryer Fallert,
Oswego, Illinois
Caryl, one of the leading colorists in our field, has a wonderful ability to create magnificent illusions through color manipulation. This quilt explores the illusion of over-lapping transparent triangles. The triangles were pieced from strips of fabric that were hand-dyed in value gradations of the primary and secondary colors. As the groups of triangles were sewn together, the illusion of long vertical diamonds appeared in the background. Photo: Courtesy of the artist

107. ILLUSION #2, 1993,
DETAIL, *Caryl Bryer Fallert,*
Oswego, Illinois
In contrast to the geometry of the pieced design in *Illusion #2,* the quilting was done in a free-form, swirling, organic design using multi-colored, shiny rayon embroidery thread. The quilting softens the geometric design while adding a beautiful, textural quality. The machine quilting was done freehand with no marking on the quilt top.
Photo: Courtesy of the artist

108. AMISH NINE-PATCH, 1992, 68" x 78"
Kay Lettau, Annandale, Virginia
This historic Nine Patch pattern is set so that interest is created with
the interplay of color and quilting lines. The colors used were inspired
by an Alexander Julien necktie. Hand-quilted by Gayle Ropp of New
York City. Photo: Ken Wagner

109. AMERICAN AS MOM AND APPLE PIE, 1993, 84" x 76"
Pat Milne Hitchcock, Sequim, Washington
This Six-Pointed Star design began with the red center star. Pat likes to
have large areas of open space for the textural effect of quilting. The quilt-
ing diagram, from *Lady's Circle Editor's Choice Patchwork Quilts*, Volume 1,
Number 1, Summer 1980, is credited to Virginia Poling. Pieced by the
English paper-piecing technique and hand-quilted. Photo: Ken Wagner

110. BLUE AND GRAY MARINER'S COMPASS, 1991, 86" x 104"
Kay Lettau, Annandale, Virginia
This high-contrast quilt combines the traditional pieced block
Mariner's Compass with Kay's original appliqué border design. Kay's
exquisite quilting accentuates the circular Mariner's Compass shape.
She has repeated a portion of her border motif in the body of the
quilt, bringing harmony to the two sections of the quilt. The blocks
were hand-pieced and then appliquéd onto the white background.
Photo: Ken Wagner

Enhancing Through Texture—The Quilting Line

Texture is one of the elements of design. For a painter, texture is created primarily through brush strokes. For a quilter, it is most often attained with quilting stitches. Thus, the quilting lines are our means of developing texture in our medium. Let your mind be open to the limitless ideas possible for quilted textural designs.

The quilting line as texture works in conjunction with the rest of the design elements, either adding details, strengthening the design statement, bringing further unity, or adding needed contrast.

While constructing your pieced or appliquéd design, write down any thoughts you have about how you may use the quilting line to promote textural details and how it may enhance your overall design. Don't disregard any ideas simply because they seem silly, different, or unattainable. Also, don't worry about your ability to capture the essence of your ideas. Whatever you can conceive in your mind, you can accomplish, if you have the desire.

Force yourself to go past the obvious when developing your quilting design. Look beyond quilting around individual pattern pieces. Consider the entire quilt as a whole entity with great linear potential, rather than as a group of individual blocks. Search for unexpected ways you can connect different parts of your design.

Think about these possibilities: Can you use quilting lines to draw the viewer's eye from one part of the quilt to another? Can you enhance or suggest movement? Can you create volume? Can you strengthen your design by adding more detail through the quilting line? Can you create the impression of spatial differences?

Realize that quilting lines give you the opportunity to increase your design's power and interest if you treat them as more than an afterthought. Be courageous. Dare to be dynamic. Certainly, take risks. Opting to attempt a new visual design through quilting will increase your creative energy, and excitement will increase. Give yourself permission to go beyond the expected. Work in small steps, allowing for growth with each new project.

If you have not determined how to quilt your design by the time the construction phase is complete, hang the piece on the wall for several days. From a distance, study the design several times each day. Jot down every idea that comes to your mind, whether you think it is good or not. Eventually you will have several ideas floating around; they may all be excellent options. In the end, you will have to decide which idea to use. Sometimes you may choose to combine two or more ideas.

QUILTING—MORE THAN JUST A LINE

Quilting lines can create details, movement, emotional feelings, and contrast. Line can be very important in your design. Different lines promote a wide variety of effects, depending on their direction, their proximity to each other, and their shapes. Examples of tremendous quilting applications are illustrated in scores of quilts included in this book. You may enjoy observing some of these differences with the following quilts:

Quilting Lines and Depth

Depth can be accentuated through quilting lines, as shown in *Jade Bay* (Photo 92). Not only do the quilting lines make the rocks look realistic, but also they create depth in both sky and water. Quilting lines were also used to create linear perspective with *Springtime in the Valley* (Photo 2). In *Dimensions of Dawn* (Photo 104), the quilting lines enhance depth uniquely with the strong variation of quilting designs. *Changing Times* (Photo 111 on the next page) uses quilting to create two planes.

Quilting Lines and Movement

Quilting lines can promote movement, as Janice Richards has done in *Tribute to Tippi Hedren* (Photo 40). Her swirling quilting lines create the effect of birds flying in the wind.

Quilting Lines and Contrast

Sometimes quilting lines provide *contrast*. Beth Gilbert's quilting in *Age of Aquarius* (Photo 105) adds both interest and intrigue. The foreground quilting gives the impression of movement and depth. The background stippling is completely unexpected and really accentuates the design. The contrast of the two styles creates a dynamic statement.

Contrast was used in *Melodious Wave* (Photo 5) to enhance the curving wave. Although the first instinct was to make the background quilting lines reiterate the wave, I sensed it would be too repetitious. While constructing this quilt, I kept visualizing strong linear lines coming from a point beyond the quilt; this is the design I chose to use. To mark the lines, I taped the quilt to the floor. Then I marked a place on the floor from which all quilting lines would radiate. With a 48" ruler and pencil, I marked the lines on the quilt, being certain that each line originated from my floor marking.

Quilting Line and Other Effects

Sometimes quilting lines are used to *visually soften* a vibrant design. Caryl Fallert's magnificent quilting in *Illusion 2* (Photos 106 and 107) does this. The fabric design, made with hand-dyed fabrics, is vibrant and strong with its linear color play. The intricate, curved quilting design subtly softens the intensity and beautifully complements the overall design. Caryl has increased her quilt's beauty by expertly changing the thread colors as the colors on the quilt top move along the surface. This is an exquisitely quilted work of art.

QUILTING LINES TO ENHANCE UNITY

Often the quilting line is the major purveyor of unity. This is particularly important when your quilt's design contains isolated motifs throughout the surface. When this occurs, the quilting line's premier duty is to bring the design together with unifying details. An example of this is Kay Lettau's *Blue and Gray Mariner's Compass* quilt (Photo 110). Another example of using the quilting lines to unify the design is Pat Hitchcock's quilt (Photo 109).

QUILTING LINES ADDING INTEREST AND DETAIL

Quilting lines can add interest and detail. Kay Lettau's *Amish Nine Patch* (Photo 108) does this while using the quilting lines to connect the various isolated designs in the quilt, bringing them together visually.

BEING RESPONSIVE TO THE DESIGN'S NEEDS

Quilting lines should fit the specific needs of the particular design. Prolific quilting is absolutely necessary for some designs; at other times, a massive amount of quilting is simply a matter of choice. Sometimes the quilting line's greatest power lies in its sparseness. It's important, then, to learn to assess your design's needs accurately.

For example, Charlotte Andersen's *Don't Go Gentle* (Photo 71) is a wonderful example of effectively using minimal quilting to help create a powerfully emotional quilt. More quilting would have diminished its overall visual impact. In contrast, Joy Baaklini's *Compass Rose* (Photo 76) combines exquisite quilting texture with its open areas and waves to enhance the center Mariner's Compass. Both of these quilts are visually successful; each quiltmaker made the best choice for her quilt.

Many quilts included in this book are noteworthy for impressive textural effects achieved through quilting. Studying them will help you see what the individual quiltmaker was attempting to accomplish with the quilting. Note, too, the differences in style.

111. CHANGING TIMES, 1984, 21" x 49"
Joen Wolfrom, Fox Island, Washington
Scale was not considered while making this quilt. Consequently, *Changing Times* stops before the design has a chance to evolve. By expanding the quilt, a more successful design would have developed, allowing scale to be in better visual agreement. Quilting adds dimension, bringing into play two planes. Photo: Ken Wagner

INDIVIDUAL PREFERENCES

Whether to quilt or not is an individual preference. Some quilts and textile art have no quilting on them. Often, texture and interest have been created by other means. For instance, several very beautiful quilts included in this book have not been quilted. Karen Perrine's *Forest Flowing* (Photo 69), Rosemary Guttler's quilts (Photos 19 and 75), and Erika Odemer's stunning Log Cabin quilt (Photo 58) are examples. These quilts are all superb artworks. Each person made the choice not to quilt her work. Each one believed her design was best served by eliminating this step. This is a personal decision that should not be questioned.

BEYOND THE QUILTING DESIGN— GETTING PRACTICAL

Thread Color Choices

One of my hand-quilting idiosyncrasies, or trademarks, is changing the color of my thread as the fabric colors change underneath. I am excited about the textural effect that the quilting stitch gives. For me, it is distracting to see an incongruous thread color. Thus with few exceptions, I choose to match thread colors with fabric colors.

I begin my quilting by threading each colored thread on its own needle. For some quilts I may have only one or two threaded at any one time, because their area of coverage is so great. However, in a small quilt with many quick color changes, I thread all the needles first, so I don't have to do it in the middle of my quilting. It takes only a little more time to pick up another needle and quilt with it.

When you change the quilting thread throughout the quilt top, you may see this thread change on the back. It usually is subtle and only noticeable with close inspection. If you think the thread color change on the back may bother you, simply use a multi-colored print for your backing fabric.

In *Setting Sun* (Photos 101 and 102), I used two or three different yellow threads for quilting the sun. The navy, steel blue, and powder blue land elements each needed one thread color to match their particular colorings. The farthest mountain range called for three different gray-valued threads. In the small wall quilt *Reflections on the Sound* (Photo 103), each colored log had its own thread color; so I used 15 assorted colors.

Machine Quilting Thread

For machine quilting I use transparent thread, which allows the fabric colors to come through the stitches. I use this thread in both the bobbin and top stitching. I do not change the tension of my sewing machine when I quilt, but I do slightly enlarge my stitch size. Additionally, I change to a smaller needle (size 60 or 70) to accommodate the thinner thread.

ACTIVITIES AND EXTENDED LEARNING:

1. Study your past quilts. Is there a prescribed way you quilt most of your designs? If so, what do you think the leading factor has been in working in this manner? At quilt exhibits, study other quilters' methods of quilting. Learn what types of quilting lines please and excite you.

2. Hang one of your past quilts on the wall for a week. Gaze at it several times a day. Try to visualize different ways you might have quilted it. (Remember, there is *no one right way.*) Consider some of the ideas listed in Activities 3 and 4 to start your brain flowing. Every time an idea enters your mind, write it down or sketch it. See if you can come up with at least five ideas in a week. When a week has passed, study your sketches and notes. Choose the quilting idea you like the best. Keep all of your sketches and written notes in a file for future use.

To further stimulate your creative thinking, each week put up another quilt and begin the process again—until you run out of quilts. You will find ideas flow more quickly as you gain experience creating imaginary design lines for texture. It should be an enjoyable activity.

If time is not a problem, before quilting on any current project, allow the quilt top to hang on the wall for several days or a week. Again, gaze at the quilt several times a day. Write or sketch all quilting ideas. Choose the quilting design that most excites you.

3. In the next year, plan to make several quilt projects that use the quilting line as an avid member of the design team. For each project, plan to use the quilting line as an avenue to do one of the following: a) to strengthen the design; b) to promote unity in the design; c) to bring contrast to the design; or d) to add details.

4. Remember that the quilting line can enhance a certain mood or suggest an idea (see Chapter 2). Play with the idea of using line to create different moods or illusions in your future quilts. With new projects, attempt to do one of the following through the quilting lines: a) create volume; b) create depth or perspective; c) create movement; d) create excitement; e) create calmness; or f) lead the viewers' eyes from one part of the quilt to another.

112. CLOSE TO HOME, 1992, 69" x 80"
Narrows Connection Quilt Guild: Gig Harbor Peninsula, Longbranch Peninsula, Fox Island, and Tacoma, Washington
This sampler quilt was the guild's tenth anniversary quilt. The theme, Washington State, was a major unifying factor throughout the quilt. Most block pictures were original designs by their makers. For some, *Quilter's News-letter Magazine* was the design source (*i.e.* tulips, trees). Although members were at liberty to use a wide variety of fabrics, green vegetation set against blue water and sky were the blocks' main color unifiers. Collection of Helen Newlands. Photo: Ken Wagner

113. UNDER THE STORM, 1991, 98" x 98"
Caryl Bryer Fallert, Oswego, Illinois
The design for this quilt was based on the traditional block Storm at Sea. This scrap quilt was made with Caryl's leftover strips from projects done in 1989. She sorted her fabrics by color and value before beginning. The border beautifully supports the major design elements. To continue the quilt's theme, the quilting was done in fish and water patterns. Schools of fantasy fish swim from the upper right corner to the lower left corner of the quilt. The spaces between the fish are filled with water patterns. Since she wanted the fish to show, Caryl chose a medium-valued gray thread to quilt against the dark and light fabrics. Photo: Courtesy of the artist

114. CLOSE TO HOME: THE VILLAGE, 1992, DETAIL
Ginny Sands, Lakebay, Washington
Washington State is filled with small communities set among the rolling hills and trees. Photo: Ken Wagner

116. CLOSE TO HOME: HARBORSCAPE, 1992, DETAIL
Janice Ohlson Richards, Vaughn, Washington
The small picturesque fishing village of Gig Harbor is nestled at the bottom of steep hills, which merge into Gig Harbor Bay. Mount Rainier makes a beautiful backdrop for the fleet of fishing boats, fishing shacks, and surrounding forests. Photo: Ken Wagner

115. CLOSE TO HOME: CLAM DIGGING ON THE SOUND, 1992, DETAIL
Helen Newlands, Gig Harbor, Washington
Native Washingtonians nostalgically look forward to clam digging on the beaches of Puget Sound. Photo: Ken Wagner

117. BALTIMORE BY MOONLIGHT, 1993, 35" x 35"
Susan Duffield, Sidney, British Columbia, Canada
This miniature Baltimore Album quilt was machine-appliquéd The border allows open space for the eye to rest, while its design application brings interest and harmony. The center heart and lower left blocks are from Elly Sienkiewicz's *Baltimore Beauties and Beyond, Volume 1*. The remaining blocks were created by Susan's experimentation with folded paper designs. Using the same variegated fabric throughout this small quilt visually simplifies the intricate design. Photo: Gary McKinstry, Victoria, British Columbia, Canada

118. NAKED LADIES, 1992, 17" x 17"
Mary Ann Rush, Fairfax, Virginia
In this intriguing Pineapple Log Cabin quilt, Mary Ann has created a beautiful border that reiterates the design's color, movement, and shape. Through her border's color application, she has also achieved the illusion of accordian-pleated folds. Mary Ann used a paper foundation technique for construction. The off-center Pineapple stamp in Lesly-Claire Greenberg's *Sewing on the Line* was used for her drafting. Photo: Lloyd Wolf

119. MIDNIGHT SUN, 1993, 87" x 87"
Judy Sogn, Seattle, Washington
Judy is well known for creating stunning original quilts using traditional patterns as her inspiration. In *Midnight Sun*, Judy started with the Broken Star pattern. She heightened the illusion of a continuous ribbon of light surrounding the central star by adding sections to the design while eliminating other areas. Judy brought the design elements into play beautifully, while keeping balance and harmony. The central design remains the major focus of this design, while the border reiterates color and shape, emphasizing unity and closure. Pieced and appliquéd. Photo: Dennis Sogn

120. TREASURES FROM OUR PAST INSPIRE OUR FUTURE 1994, 43" x 43"
Anita Krug, West Lafayette, Indiana
Anita challenged herself to design a quilt using the two traditional
block patterns Log Cabin and Pineapple Log Cabin. With the help of a
computer, she moved these patterns across the face of the quilt surface
by gradually changing one block into the other. In order to accomplish
this, Anita created a mutated block—a Flying Geese-style Log Cabin.
Anita used full-size print-outs with light and dark colorations to do a
mock-up on the wall. After Anita was satisfied with the block placement, she printed blocks to use as a base for paper piecing. As Anita
extended her design elements into the border, she muted the colors, so
as not to overpower the design. Her border beautifully brings closure
and unity to the overall design. Photo: Ken Wagner

121. RADIANCE EVOLVED, 1991, 65" x 99"
Linda Helme Hillan, Brooklyn Park, Minnesota
This lovely quilt was based on the traditional block Star of Many
Points. Linda made major changes to the block before beginning its fabric construction. First she drafted the block to fit into a 6" square. Then
she changed its corners and added a border to the block. Although she
began with a traditional pattern, her innovative block-design play has
created an entirely different look. Hand-pieced and hand-quilted.
Photo: Ken Wagner

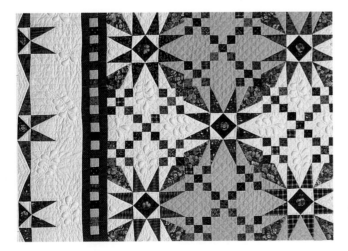

122. IRISH EYES, 1991, DETAIL
Irma Gail Hatcher, Conway, Arkansas
The design and beautiful quilting in Irma Gail's *Irish Eyes* can be seen
in this detailed view. The partial star motif's repetition connects the
border wonderfully with the body of the quilt. Contrast is achieved
through the border stars' incomplete patterning. Photo: George Chambers

123. IRISH EYES, 1991, 72" x 74"
Irma Gail Hatcher, Conway, Arkansas
This lovely two-block traditional quilt was made from two pieced
blocks: Irish Chain and Pineapple Star (variation). Photo: George
Chambers, Little Rock, Arkansas

Chapter Nine

Designing Spectacular Traditional Quilts—
Setting the Stage

At any quilt gathering, we see the total spectrum of quilts, from the splendidly spectacular to the very nice to the unremarkable, and sometimes even to the visually disastrous. It is hard work making a quilt, and it takes considerable time, energy, and money. Naturally, we want all of our quilts to be beautiful; it is a great disappointment when they don't turn out as nicely as we wish. A spectacular quilt is rarely the result of a haphazard plan. It is more often the culmination of good planning, wise design application, solid technical application, and the self-confidence to rely on one's intuitive spontaneity at a moment's notice.

Traditional quilts with design problems tend to fall into the same few categories. Almost always, these problems are caused by inattention to basic design practices. Nearly all could have been eliminated during the quilt's planning stages. This chapter's focus is on the first two steps—beginning with a good plan and making wise choices that will enhance a quilt's visual appeal.

CREATING BALANCE—
THE EYE'S NATURAL FOCUS

Our eyes are sensitive to visual balance. We are uncomfortable when a quilt is visually imbalanced. We need to stand back and observe our designs as they progress so we can make changes as needed.

Bed Quilts

BALANCE WITH AN UNEVEN NUMBER OF BLOCKS

As a rule, a better design is created when the number of blocks is horizontally uneven. This means most bed quilts will have three, five, seven, or nine blocks across the *top* of the bed, depending on the bed's size and the block's size. Any additional blocks and borders used to hang down the sides of the bed are add-ons. These extras should always be figured in with the total design. However, it is important to know what your design will look like on the bed top, so plan that first. Then create the side design so the two units combine to create a beautiful quilt with design unity.

Figures 9-1 and 9-2 show two quilt designs for the top of a bed (without borders and sides), both using the Evening Star pattern. Notice one top has five horizontal blocks, while the other has four blocks across. Because our eyes tend to focus on the vertical middle, with the uneven top (Figure 9-1) we focus on the middle star row; with the even-block design, our focus is on the midpoint background (Figure 9-2).

Figure 9-1. Because our eyes focus naturally on the midpoint of a design, most block settings are best with an uneven number of horizontal blocks.

Figure 9-2. Often when the number of horizontal blocks is an even number, our eyes naturally focus on the background instead of the foreground design. This happens because the midpoint of the

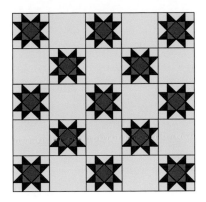

Figure 9-3. When blocks are alternated with background blocks (plain blocks), the visual weight is better distributed with an uneven number of horizontal blocks.

Figure 9-4. Alternate block designs can give an overall lopsided or imbalanced appearance when the blocks are set in an even number horizontally.

If you alternate pieced or appliquéd blocks with plain blocks, there is an additional balance problem with an even number of horizontal blocks. As you can see in Figure 9-3, the weight is evenly distributed throughout the quilt with the uneven number. However, with an even number of blocks (Figure 9-4), the quilt looks lopsided.

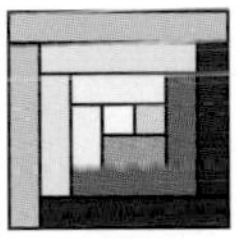

BALANCE WITH AN EVEN NUMBER OF BLOCKS HORIZONTALLY

Not all blocks react positively to the *uneven balance rule*. Some blocks require an even number of blocks across the quilt to make a balanced design. A good example is the Log Cabin Barn-Raising pattern (Figures 9-5 and 9-6). This would appear unbalanced if created with an uneven number of blocks (Figures 9-7).

BLOCK NUMBER AND BED MEASUREMENTS

Before beginning your quilt, determine how many blocks you want in your design. To do this, you need to know the mattress size for the quilt's bed. See the chart on the next page:

Figure 9-5. Some traditional designs need an even number of horizontal blocks to create a balanced design. Traditional Log Cabin designs belong to this group.

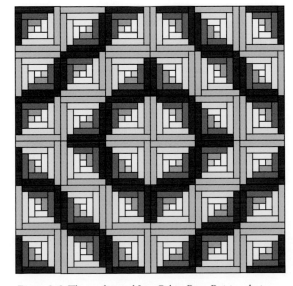

Figure 9-6. The traditional Log Cabin Barn-Raising design needs an even number of horizontal blocks to create a pleasing design.

Figure 9-7. When the traditional Log Cabin Barn-Raising pattern is set with an uneven number of horizontal blocks, the design loses its appeal. It is imbalanced.

Type of Mattress	W/L Inches
Crib, six year	27" x 52"
Twin, regular	39" x 75"
Twin, long	39" x 80"
Double, regular	54" x 75"
Double, long	54" x 80"
Queen	60" x 80"
King, regular	76" x 80"
King, California	72" x 84"
King, dual	78" x 80"
King, water bed	72" x 84"

To determine how many blocks you need for the top of your bed, you must first decide if the block pattern you are going to use will be best with an uneven or an even number of blocks across the top.

It is almost always true that using only three blocks across the top of a bed makes the blocks too large to be visually pleasing. Five or seven blocks are potentially the best amount of odd-numbered blocks to use for this top area. If your design calls for an even number of blocks across the top, four would be the minimum. Six or eight would probably be the maximum amount.

To figure the block size, divide the mattress width by the number of horizontal blocks you plan to use for that width. The quotient will be your block size. If you are going to have five blocks across the top of a 60" mattress (queen-size bed), you will use 12" blocks. If you chose to use seven blocks, then each would be $8\frac{5}{8}$" (you could round it off to $8\frac{1}{2}$").

Wall Quilts: Design, Focus, and Balance

Wall quilts are particularly sensitive to visual balance, because they hang on the wall for everyone to see clearly. Once you have chosen the block design for your quilt, it is extremely important to find the setting that will be most pleasing. This depends on the pattern you have chosen.

Like people, not all blocks act the same in similar circumstances. To create the best design possible with your selected pattern, do a little pre-playing with several paper blocks. Through this activity you may decide to change your block selection, or you may find a setting that particularly excites you.

Notice that the Evening Star pattern (Figure 9-8) has a very static feeling, whereas the Wyoming Valley block appears to have movement (Figure 9-12). In all likelihood, multiple Wyoming Valley blocks will work together in a more interesting design than the motionless Evening Star block. You will have much better ideas about which design will work best for you, if you allow yourself time to play with small paper blocks (2" size).

Figure 9-8. The Evening Star block needs no other block to clarify its design. This characteristic may be a clue to a static pattern. Notice how the focus changes as the number of horizontal blocks increases in Figures 9-9 to 9-11.

THE EYES' FOCUS—
THE PROBLEMATIC FOUR-BLOCK DESIGN

In most traditional wall quilts, your eyes are drawn to the center of the quilt, regardless of the size or design. This almost always presents a problem when you use only four blocks for the quilt's design. Usually the center area of four united blocks is a large background space. The four-block Evening Star wall design (Figure 9-9) is such a setting. Our eyes go right to the large square of background in the center. In fact, we must force our eyes to shift to any of the four stars. Even as we force our eyes outward, they still want to move back to the center area.

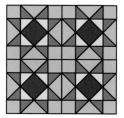

Figure 9-9. When four blocks are set together, our eyes focus on the center background rather than the foreground design. We must force our eyes to look outward to see stars.

To make up for this design flaw, many quilters intricately quilt the center background of these quilts. This only accentuates the background area even more, so the background ends up competing with the foreground design.

There is little you can do with this design problem, unless of course, you choose to add more blocks. When two more blocks are added to the design (Figure 9-10), the eyes still focus on the center area, but this time the focal point is two star blocks. Probably the most pleasing of these three small quilt arrangements would be the nine-block design (Figure 9-11). It has just enough blocks to allow the design to take shape. Notice how your eyes go automatically to the center star in this placement.

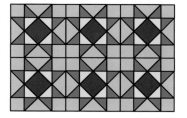

Figure 9-10. When an uneven number of horizontal blocks is used, our eyes focus on the middle blocks. This allows the background to take its rightful position in a secondary role.

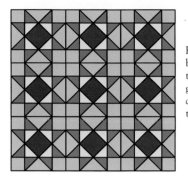

Figure 9-11. With a nine-block design, our eyes focus on the center block, the background is secondary, and the design has enough room to establish itself.

Figure 9-14. With the Wyoming Valley pattern, the six-block setting may be the least pleasing option because our eyes' natural tendency is to move to the center area. However, they are strongly distracted by the two star patterns on either side. The center, then, does not have a strong-enough design to hold the eyes' attention.

A FOUR-BLOCK DESIGN WITH DIFFERENT RESULTS

Some patterns surprise us when four blocks are combined. Wyoming Valley (Figure 9-12) is such a design. When four blocks are put together, a new central star design evolves (Figure 9-13).

With the nine-block design of Wyoming Valley, the original design and the uniting stars are both visible (Figure 9-15). This could be really very nice, as long as you emphasize the block design and have the inner stars remain as accents. If the stars were emphasized, they would have to be very bold to overtake the visual strength of the original design.

Figure 9-12. Wyoming Valley is undefined when gazing at just one block. This is usually a clue to an interesting block pattern. This nine-patch pattern moves outward at its diagonal corners.

Figure 9-13. Placing four Wyoming Valley blocks together creates a surprise center. By careful fabric selection, this could be a dynamic wall quilt.

Figure 9-15. By adding another horizontal row to the Wyoming Valley design, our eyes now focus on the middle block. If we have correctly placed our fabrics in the design, our eyes should be satisfied with the central design. If, however, the corner stars pull out of the design because of strong coloring, then causing the eyes to focus on them, the design's success will be diminished. If the four stars do not compete, a beautiful design will result.

Surprisingly, in Wyoming Valley the four-block setting seems much more pleasing than the six-block setting (Figure 9-14). With the latter, the eye focuses on the center area that borders the two middle stars. However, since the stars are quite strong, they also want attention. It results in the stars and the small center area competing against each other, to the design's detriment.

Know Your Design Before You Start

It is almost impossible to know how a block will interact with other blocks by only seeing a one-block example from a book. Some blocks look wonderful in isolation, but are not quite as pleasing in a group setting. Other blocks do not have great appeal alone, but when they are put together as a group, the results are fantastic.

Don't presume to know how your quilt blocks will go together unless you have actually seen a quilt using the identical blocks. Quilting is too time-intensive and costly for guesswork designing. So begin each quilt with an *initial block-play paper study*. This exercise may take a few hours of your time (depending on how far away you are from a copy machine), but it is well worth the effort in the end—and it is actually fun to do.

Initial Block-Play Paper Study

Make four or five copies of your block on one sheet of paper. In general, 2" (5cm to 6cm) blocks should do well for this block play. Duplicate your page of blocks enough times so you have 20 to 30 blocks to play with. Then cut the blocks apart. (I do not color my blocks during this stage, but you may wish to do so.)

Arrange the blocks in the way you first envision them as a quilt. Then rearrange the blocks in several different ways. Notice what happens in the different design arrangements. What are the design's strengths? What are its weaknesses? Do you think the block combination has the potential to make a beautiful quilt? Or do you now have reservations about this block's design potential?

Taking time to work with the paper blocks before you actually begin working on the quilt eliminates possible surprises and disappointments. If you are not happy with any of your first block arrangements, play with the blocks until you come up with an idea that pleases you. If nothing really excites you, select another pattern and begin the process again. At this point, if the *paper play* design doesn't meet your expectations, you should be happy that you didn't make the original quilt.

Pattern Variations

Patterns are like people. They react differently to situations. Some patterns are best as the center of attraction, such as in a medallion quilt (Figures 9-16 and 9-17). Other block patterns do not have enough interest or visual strength to form the center of a medallion. Capital T, a simple block pattern, is such an example (Figure 9-18).

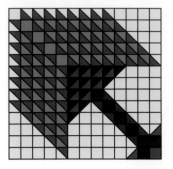

Figure 9-16. If you want to create a medallion quilt or a round-robin quilt, be certain to choose a block with strong design potential as your center focus.

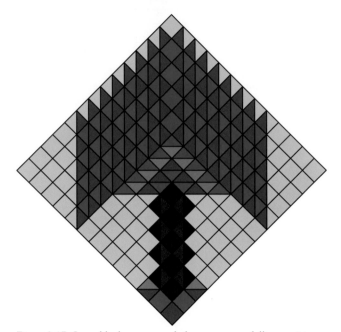

Figure 9-17. Some blocks are naturals for a center medallion position. A successful design should be able to attract the eye immediately. Tree of Life set on point is such a pattern.

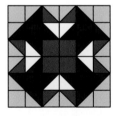

Figure 9-18. Some block designs, like Capital T, do not have strong enough design features to be positioned as a central focus in a quilt. They are easily overwhelmed by multiple borders.

A large group of block patterns may touch each other at the blocks' edges, but they really do not interact with their identical counterparts. Often, they present a rather static appearance. Braced Star, an easy block pattern, reacts in this manner (Figure 9-19).

Some blocks actually can override their rigidity even though their design may be fairly static in nature. For instance, All Hallows (Figure 9-20) gives us a visual clue with its diagonal trapezoids forming a lattice with the adjoining blocks. The breaking up of the corner pieces sug-

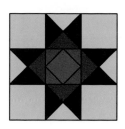
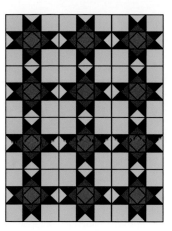

Figure 9-19. Patterns that are clearly defined within the block often result in a predictable or static appearance when placed with other identical blocks. Braced Star, like many other patterns, gives a static, stable appearance in a traditional setting.

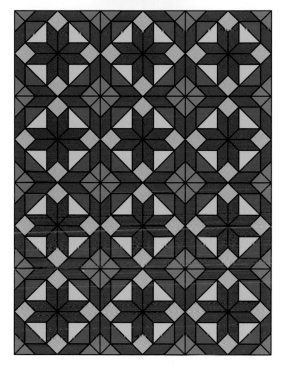

Figure 9-20. Some blocks have illusionary possibilities when placed with identical blocks. In All Hallows, the illusion of depth can be promoted. By incorporating illusions in your design, you can change an otherwise static block into an intriguing design.

gests possible illusionary play with other blocks. However, it's difficult to see the design's potential until you begin playing with the paper blocks.

There are many design options with All Hallows. The one shown here has a spatial quality to it. The stars seem to be behind a lattice structure. This spatial relationship could be even more interesting if no two blocks used exactly the same fabrics. If you wanted the stars to move forward and become the primary focus, the values and scales for the two different spatial designs would have to be reversed.

USING THE BLOCK'S DESIGN CLUES

Study the design you have chosen. Does your block look self-sufficient? If it does, it may lean toward a static appearance (Figures 9-8 and 9-19). Does the design feel incomplete? Is it difficult to see how the design will evolve by looking at one block (Figure 9-20)? If so, it may create a fascinating overall design.

Strong diagonal bands moving toward the four corners of a block are a key to an interlocking connection between blocks. The same holds true for strong centrally located vertical and horizontal bands. Many of these patterns are five-patch or seven-patch designs. Other blocks are more subtle in their interlocking clues. They have triangular points meeting at the corners.

Some patterns are quite clunky or heavy, and will be no better in multiples. Considerable changes must be made before these kinds of blocks evolve into beautiful designs. If you want to work with a block such as this, explore many design possibilities. You may find an innovative block arrangement with interesting color and fabric selection that will work into a great quilt.

BORDER ENHANCEMENT— AN AREA OF GREAT CONCERN

The purpose of a border is to support, enhance, complete an effect, or give visual closure. A border should play a similar role in a quilt to harmony's role in a song. The successful composer never forgets the difference between the melody and harmony; the successful quilter never allows the border to play the dominant role in her quilt.

A border is not the place to introduce a new idea or image to a quilt; it is a time for reflection and support. This closing feature of the design simply reiterates elements and mirrors part of the overall design. This reflection may be done through color, fabric selection, shapes, and/or pattern choices. The borders of *Irish Eyes* (Photos 122 and 123), *Midnight Sun* (Photo 119), and *Naked Ladies* (Photo 118) all repeat design shapes and colors

If we have to force our eyes to move from the border into the body of the quilt, or if our eyes bounce back and forth from the design to the border, the border treatment is unsuccessful. It has become so powerful that it is visually competing with the design.

There may be many reasons why a quilt border takes over the design focus. One very simple reason is inadequate planning. For instance, if you have made all the quilt blocks, and then find the quilt is not big enough, you might decide to make up the difference by adding more borders—or making bigger borders. This seems like a simple solution to a size problem. Since this solution usually results in a less beautiful quilt, it makes better sense to plan the size of both the quilt's main body and the border before beginning the project.

Guidelines for Border Designs

UNITY OF COLOR

The colors selected for the border should also appear in the body of the quilt (Photos 117, 118, 119, 120, 122, and 123). This is an extremely important rule, and there are very few reasons for dismissing this guideline. If a new color is introduced in the border, our eyes are immediately drawn to it. So, rather than helping unify the quilt, a new color creates competition. This can overpower the other colors used in the body of the quilt.

If you decide to introduce a new color in the border, it must be done with great care. An experienced quilter with an eye for color may be able to use a new color in the border without it affecting the work negatively. Without this intuitive ability, however, we jeopardize the beauty of our quilts by doing so.

It is always a wise choice to use your quilt's dominant color as the primary hue in the border. Additionally, you can use the secondary color in a similar position in the border, while one of the quilt's accent colors plays a minor role. This plan gives unity to the overall color statement.

Some quilt borders are pieced in such a way that they reiterate almost all the colors in the quilt's body. These borders can be very effective (Photo 28). Often they are set apart by a very thin narrow strip or piping as a visual introduction to the border. When you use multiple colors, they should be well controlled. Rarely are the colors thrown haphazardly into the border with no regard to what has been going on in the main design.

UNITY OF FABRICS

Like color, fabric use has a similar set of rules. With regard to print fabrics, with few exceptions, no print should go into the border that is not already in the body of the quilt. A new print placed into the border is almost always distracting, as it draws our eyes to it.

The same is true for solid-colored fabrics. A solid-colored fabric that is not in the body of the quilt generally should not be placed in the border. There is one exception to this rule, however. You can substitute a solid-colored fabric in place of a print, as long as its color closely matches the print's coloration. Thus, an emerald green solid-colored fabric can take the place of an emerald green print. However, if your eyes tend to be drawn to this new border fabric, reconsider your choice. Its value or intensity may be enough off to be distracting. In that case, replace this fabric.

People who have great color sense can get away with stretching these guidelines. However, it is wise to follow these basic rules when you are still developing your color sense. If you are talented in color and fabric manipulation, you may decide to bend the rules by including fabrics that were not used in the body of the quilt. Do so with care. Use your intuition to let you know whether it looks great or if it simply affected your quilt's design unity negatively.

UNITY OF SHAPES

If shapes are part of your border design, make certain they either repeat shapes used in the quilt's body or are portions of these shapes. If your overall design incorporates a large variety of triangles and squares, select the shapes (or parts of them) that are most dominant to repeat rather than the obscure ones.

Marie Fritz has created a wonderful border in her *Winchester Charm* quilt (Photo 77) to reiterate her design. Other excellent examples of borders using repeated shapes or motifs are *Awakenings* (Photo 22), *Southwest of Amish* (Photo 42), and *The Other Side of My Grandmother's Flower Garden* (Photo 62). *Irish Eyes* (Photo 123) is a wonderful example of using only part of a motif in the border.

The border is not the place to begin using new shapes. If, for instance, your major design incorporates a variety of triangles and squares, you would not use diamonds or circles in the border. To do so would cause the eye to move right to the border, creating competition.

UNITY OF PATTERN

Pattern and shape are closely related. When you put together a group of shapes, they form a pattern. When this pattern is repeated, you create a visual rhythm. Repeating that pattern in the border is often very pleasing. Sometimes, however, the whole pattern is too much, as it becomes too large. Therefore, choosing just a portion of the major pattern to use in the border is a clever way to create unity (Photos 122-123).

Again, a border is not the place to bring a new pattern into play. If you do, you create competition with the body of the quilt. Then the eyes would not know where to look, and they would become as interested, or more interested, in the border as in the quilt's design.

SIZE OF SHAPES

There must be a relationship between the size of the pieces in the border and the size of the pieces in the quilt's body. No shape in the border should be bigger than any shape within the body of the quilt. For instance, if the largest shape in the design is a 3" half-square triangle, do not put 4" half-square triangles in the border. They will be out of proportion to the rest of the quilt; consequently, this will detract from your design.

Many quilters use smaller shapes in their border than in the body of the quilt. Do so with care. If in doing so you pleasingly repeat a pattern from the inner design, it will probably relate well. If, for instance, you have a quilt primarily made of squares, you may checkerboard your pattern in the border by using four squares to every square in the main design.

If you make the shapes smaller, there should be an obvious relationship to the design and/or to the shape itself. For instance, if you want smaller triangles in the border, don't make them just a little smaller. They will appear as if they were made by mistake. Instead, make them an understandable ratio, like one-half smaller or one-fourth smaller.

SIZE OF THE BORDER

A plaguing problem for quilters is knowing how large to make a border. Many borders outgrow their design. This is especially true with multiple borders. Somehow, the border's purpose is forgotten. It is no longer an enhancement but a distraction to the design.

If the border is out of proportion to the rest of the design, it seriously competes with the design, often overwhelming it. When this happens, the border becomes dominant; the quilt design no longer is the most important feature in the design. It then plays an insignificant role.

Borders that Move the Design Outward

Some quiltmakers use innovative methods to border their quilts. This is particularly useful for picture quilts. Designs that are stopped by a small border introduction, such as a narrow band or piping, and then continue in a subtle fashion can be very effective. Excellent examples include *Jade Bay* (Photo 92), *Gradation* (Photo 28), *When East Meets West* (Photo 15), and *Journey Home* (Photo 30). Notice that some are much more subtle than others in this blending of border and design.

Additionally, some quiltmakers use the border to develop their design further through visual suggestion (Photos 66 and 68). The border of *Baltimore by Moonlight* (Photo 117) expands the appliqué design theme and develops the quiltmaker's focus. Susan Duffield, the creator, has made certain the border does not overpower the major

design by minimizing the border shapes. She has also very carefully kept the color and fabric use the same.

Charlotte Andersen's *Don't Go Gentle* (Photo 71) is very dramatic in its simplicity. It closes the picture off beautifully with a subtle use of fabrics. The tiny plaid and check border fabric cleverly reiterates the most striking fabric in the quilt—her father's jacket. Caryl Fallert's *Under the Storm* (Photo 113), Gloria Hansen's *Awakenings* (Photo 22), Marion Marias' *Spring in the Valley* (Photo 14), and Anita Krug's *Treasures From Our Past Inspire Our Future* (Photo 120) have used fabrics that are more muted than those in the body of the quilt. This effective treatment often gives the illusion of transparency.

QUILTS WITH SPECIAL DESIGN CONSIDERATIONS

We want every traditional quilt to live up to its highest expectation. Certain types of quilts, however, have unique problems that continue to plague us. Usually these difficulties are directly related to the design elements and principles, particularly unity, proportion, scale, contrast, and variation. Some styles, like round-robin, sampler, and medallion quilts, are especially sensitive to problems. The remainder of this chapter focuses on the concerns we must attend to when creating these quilts.

Multiple Block Quilt

In a multiple block quilt, the border size should relate to the divisions within the block. Therefore, if you are working with nine-patch blocks, a good width for the border would be the measurement of one-third of a block's size. Maximum size would be one-half block. Making the border wider can present a proportional problem, as it tends to create visual competition with the design.

Medallion Quilts

By definition, a medallion is an oval or circular design. In the quilt world, we have a broader interpretation, calling any quilt with a large central design, surrounded by borders, a medallion quilt. In most medallion quilts, this central design is square, rectangular, circular, or oval. Examples of beautiful medallion quilts include those in Photos 11, 56, 59, 76, and 88. Study these quilts to see how they worked within the following guidelines.

Medallion quilts have the potential to be both exquisite and eye-catching. To achieve success, however, planning is essential. This does not mean you must follow a rigid formula or have a "set in stone" master plan. However, because medallion quilts incorporate a center design with several surrounding borders, these quilts can be fraught with design problems.

Since medallion quilts are radial designs by nature, the central motif is best if it also appears to radiate from the center. This reiteration of central radiation gives energy and natural balance to the quilt. So choose your central motif carefully, trying to select one that will enhance the radial balance that a medallion quilt naturally elicits.

Although there is no set formula for how large a medallion quilt's central design area should be, there should be a visual balance between it and the borders, if the quilt is going to be visually successful. Naturally, this varies with each design, as well as the fabrics, colors, and values used.

Remember that a circular medallion generally works best in a square format (Photo 88), while a rectangular medallion design is almost always better reiterating the rectangular format (Photos 11 and 59).

Two definite problems plague medallion quilts. The first is dwarfing the central motif with an overabundance or oversizing of its multiple borders. The second troublesome problem with many medallion quilts is lack of unity.

MULTIPLE BORDER OVERKILL

Many medallion quilts have too many borders. These borders, rather than the central motif, then control the quilt's design. As a guideline, keep the central design area the largest section of your quilt.

The total width of one side of a medallion border should be less than the width of the quilt's central area. Actually, I believe it is more pleasing, visually, to keep each side's border area less than half the size of the central area. By doing this you can better control the quilt's visual balance, while keeping the major interest within the body of the quilt—as it should be.

LACK OF UNITY

The second major problem is caused by lack of unity within the design elements. Borders often show no relationship to the medallion design, and they often have no similarity to each other. Because of this incongruity, the quilt's design flow is totally interrupted. When this happens, the potentially beautiful quilt evaporates into a visually busy, distracting sight.

When you create a medallion quilt, it is most important to follow all the border rules listed earlier in this chapter. The quilt's central body should introduce all the important parts: color, fabric, shapes, values, scale, direction, and patterns. These, then, will be reiterated throughout the rest of the quilt to give unity and flow. If you introduce a new color, a new shape, or a new pattern in a border, it will be distracting, drawing your eye away from the whole design and into that particular border.

Often, a medallion quilt's borders seem out-of-control. It is as if the quiltmaker wanted to put everything she knew into one quilt. When this happens, it becomes a jumbled mess. So before you start, think about what you want to do in your quilt design and how you will go about doing it. Know what elements you want to stress. Have fun bringing the different design elements into the borders in unique ways.

It may be helpful to note that a medallion quilt is similar to a symphony with its distinct movements or divisions. Even though these symphonic divisions have their own individuality, a unifying theme still runs throughout. Also, continuity and contrast exist between movements. The contrast enhances and provides interest, while the continuity provides unity. These same characteristics are also prevalent in successful medallion quilts.

Remember, however, too much contrast causes competition between the elements, the borders, and the central design area, thus destroying the overall possibility of the unity and beauty we seek. There is a delicate line between too much contrast and not enough unity.

Round-Robin Quilts

Round-robin quilts are our modern-day version of a friendship quilt. In a round-robin quilt group, each quilter begins by making her own medallion design. This may range from a simple traditional block pattern to an intricate inner design. When she finishes this portion of the quilt, she passes it on to the next person in the group. That person adds a design or border treatment to the central design. When she finishes her portion of the quilt, she sends it on to the next person. Eventually, everyone in the group has added a design area or border.

Unfortunately, round-robin quilts are particularly vulnerable to disunity. Many of these quilts lose the focus of the central design, as the borders tend to compete and win the visual dominance battle. Therefore, it is essential that the friendship group discusses the importance of both achieving visual balance and keeping the inner design's strength intact.

In a round-robin quilt, no single border should compete with the central focus or with any other border. Each additional border should enhance the others. The focus should be a combination of limited contrast and individuality, while maintaining continuity and unity.

The same rules apply to a round-robin quilt as to a medallion quilt. The central design must set the foundation for the shapes, colors, scale and proportion, direction, values, patterns, and fabrics used. The central design plays the leading role, and all else is a reiteration in some sort of visual interplay. For this reason, the inner block must not only be strong enough to hold a viewer's eye, it must have enough interest, unity, and contrast, to support the various border treatments.

The round-robin quilt is similar to a stone dropped into a pond. The succeeding ripples of wave action are based on what has come before—all beginning at the center. Thus, it is not the goal of each succeeding person to attempt to outdo any design area completed before hers. Her role, actually, is to create a border area that maintains unity with all the preceding areas of work. Most importantly, there must be a definite relationship between her area and the central design—the body of the quilt.

A most difficult task confronts the quiltmaker who creates the final border treatment. Great care must be taken here to bring everything to completion. It is that last quiltmaker's obligation to achieve visual unity. If any areas or elements are weak, it will be her duty to work toward eliminating these problems. At the very least, she should attempt to disguise any problems through clever manipulation of the elements.

THE ROUND-ROBIN QUILT OWNER'S RESPONSIBILITY

Because everything must relate visually to the center area, it behooves the quilt owner to take the time to create a beautiful, interesting central design for herself. This major focus should be well-planned. If the owner has done her work well, she will have given her friends enough leeway to create effectively both unity and contrast through the different design elements. Then her round-robin quilt will not only be fun, it will be visually beautiful.

Since every quilt's central area will be different in size and visual strength, it may be a wise plan for each quilt owner to determine how wide she wants each border treatment to be. Each quilt should have a basic visual plan for a size guideline that is determined by the central design area. This plan keeps the central focus intact and will help eliminate the border treatment getting out of control.

Landscape Quilts

Most landscape quilts do not need a border. If you put one on, it should be very subtle and follow the visual theme. It should not compete with the body of the quilt.

A landscape quilt presents a particular problem with color in the border. The sky and foreground are almost never in the same colors, so surrounding the entire quilt with the same color may be great for one area of the quilt, but too bold for another. To get around this, quilters sometimes continue the visual picture into the border. Often, they introduce its beginning with a small, thin, distinct inner border or piping (Photos 14, 30, and 92). Other quiltmakers do not put borders on their landscape quilts, as they believe them to be distracting. Usually these quilts are simply bound or professionally framed (Photos 2, 3, 69, 81, and 101; photo 138 on page 144).

Sometimes pieced blocks are set around a landscape. If there is no visual relationship between the two parts of the quilt, it can be very distracting. Thus it must be done with great care. When this border treatment is used, the pieced design should relate in scale, color, and fabric selection. Using pieced blocks that are only conceptually related seldom works visually. For instance, bordering *Setting Sun* (Photo 101) with the traditional Delectable Mountain block would be distracting. Although the block name refers to a mountain, the design would compete with the scene. For best results, there must be a visual relationship between the scene and the block design used.

Appliqué and Pieced Quilts

Many beautiful quilts use both appliqué and pieced work. When this is done effectively, these quilts frequently have a much greater impact than a quilt created from only one of these techniques (Photos 45, 59, 69, 76, and 81). Many award-winning quilts combine techniques, since it quite often results in a much richer design, if done properly.

If you wish to mix appliqué and pieced work in your quilt design, make certain one of the techniques will be dominant. The two must not compete visually with each other. The secondary technique should not be placed only incidentally within the design. It should be visually relevant, and it should be integrated into the design so that it looks like it belongs. A good guideline to follow is to repeat the use of the secondary technique at least once, so that it does not look like an add-on.

Sampler Quilts

Sampler quilts are some of the most difficult to create with beautiful visual success. It is unfortunate, then, that so many beginning quilters are asked to make these quilts. Sampler quilts are used to give beginning quiltmakers experience with a wide variety of patterns and technical applications. Since technique is the primary focus in this sampler exercise, the new quiltmaker will rarely be able to concentrate on design application.

Visual balance and unity are two important principles frequently missing in sampler quilts. It's important that no block appears too heavy or light in its placement. Appliqué blocks tend to weigh less visually than most pieced blocks. Some pieced blocks are delicate in their features, while others appear clunky. Thus, a quiltmaker must carefully manipulate colors, values, and fabrics to create an overall design where the visual weight is equally distributed throughout the surface.

Selecting a group of blocks that look good together is the first step in creating a successful sampler quilt. Don't assume that a random group will automatically work.

Additionally, consider using similar fabrics and/or colors in each block to help the eye flow from one block to the next. This should help promote unity.

GROUP SAMPLER QUILT

Making a successful group sampler quilt can be difficult, because everyone is working on her own block independently. Care must be given to fabric selection and color, since these may be the only unifying factors in the entire quilt. So ground rules must be set up in advance.

My guild made a group sampler quilt for our 10th anniversary (Photos 112, 114, 115, and 116). Thirty of us took part in this project. First, we decided our theme was Washington State. On butcher paper we divided our total quilt surface into a variety of block sizes. Some were square; others were rectangular. Some blocks were given a specific subject; others had no specifications. A few blocks were assigned to people, while everyone else selected a block of their own choosing. Each of us picked our own fabric from a large collection of hand-dyed materials.

It was challenging, but wonderfully fun, to put these blocks together. Some of our original plans had to be set aside once we began joining the blocks. A few blocks were cut up, redesigned, and then placed back into the design. Originally, we planned to have quilted lattice work between the blocks, but we found it distracting. Thus our plans changed. We were excited and pleased when it was completed. We each placed our name in a container for every hour we had worked on the quilt. Then we had a drawing to determine who would win the quilt. The happy owner is Helen Newlands, the person who had worked on the quilt the most hours.

OTHER DESIGN CONCERNS

Visually unsuccessful quilts often have no strong, unifying factor. They often have too much going on. Their "busyness" tends to confuse, rather than impress. Simple quilts can be quite powerful. They pull us in with their quiet strength of design.

Problem One:
The Distractingly Busy Quilt

Some quilts are distracting and unattractive because no unifying factor or element brings all the parts together. They lack harmony and unity. With these quilts, no consideration has been given to the functions of the design elements or the design principles. Simply, elements appear to have been thrown together, with several out-of-control. The end result is that fabrics, colors, values, and shapes all compete with each other. When this happens, there is no focus or direction. The eye has no place to rest. Every element in the quilt design fights for dominance, with visual bedlam the result.

If you think your quilt is too busy, analyze why. Is there a dominant color in your quilt? Is there a dominant color scale and/or value scale? Are your fabrics compatible? Is your design harmonic? Does it have unity?

Determine your specific problem areas. Study the concepts with which you need help. When you begin your next quilt, attempt to achieve some order in the design. Think through some of the visual parts of your quilt. If it all seems too confusing, concentrate on only one element of the design (e.g., color). Attempt to create unity and balance by concentrating on this one element.

CREATING AN EXCITING "BUSY" QUILT

It is important to note that not all busy quilts are examples of poor design. Busy quilts can be both intriguing and exciting. However, there is a knack to creating a successful "busy" quilt. These quilts are not made haphazardly or with no design control. Usually they are created by quilters who use their intuition and sensitive eyes to formulate their designs.

Thus, for the most part, successful busy quilts are still created with an adherence to design principles. These quilts will exhibit a dominant color family and value scale. Usually the design has been developed either to move our eyes across the quilt's surface or to focus on a particular part of the surface. Also, there is unity within the quilt; something holds the elements together. The design is not so disconnected that nothing seems related.

Making a successfully busy quilt takes thought and good skill. Most novice quilters do not have enough experience to pull it off. Even experienced quilters may flounder with their first attempts. This is part of the growing process. Expect to have some difficulties when creating your first intricately busy quilt.

Problem Two:
The Background Takes Over
the Dominant Role

A few quilts lack design interest, so the background takes on the dominant role. This can happen when the design area is small in comparison to the total quilt surface. The scale is wrong. At other times, it can happen if the background color (or value) is stronger than the design's hues. Remember, your foreground design should hold the premier role. The background's role is to support the design by providing balance and rest.

Check the progress of your design by standing back at least 10 feet. Make certain your main design is indeed the focus of your quilt. If it is not, analyze what is happening. Are the colors creating a problem? Does the design relate well to the background? Are the scale and proportion correct? Are the fabrics causing any problems? Are they fighting with each other? Are the background fabrics stronger than the design fabrics? Is the design fading into the background in unwanted places?

If any of these elements are causing problems, stop your progress temporarily so you can determine what needs to be done. Do not be afraid to take out parts of your quilt or make new blocks to replace others. Do whatever you can to rectify the problem before it becomes an overwhelming task. Alas, if you decide the problems cannot be rectified, then learn as much as you can from this situation, so you will not have to repeat it at a later time.

Problem Three: Putting (Almost) Everything You Know Into One Quilt

Putting almost everything you know into a quilt can give a quilt a haphazard, busy look. Each part of the design may be wonderful in itself, but together all of the parts compete too much with one another and overwhelm the surface. Don't feel it is necessary to put all your favorite techniques, designs, shapes, or colors into one quilt. Use some frugality when it comes to choices. Remember, each quilt is not the only one you will make. You will have plenty of time to experiment with all of your favorite ideas.

Round-robin quilts are particularly vulnerable to this problem. It is important to remember that there must be unity within a quilt. This is easily done through repetition of color, shape, value, and pattern throughout the entire surface area.

ACTIVITIES AND EXTENDED LEARNING:

1. Analyzing Your Past Projects

If you have past quilt projects that have been disappointing, take time to study them now. While analyzing them, consider the ideas covered in this chapter and in the earlier design chapters (Chapters 2-6). Some of the primary areas of concern are mentioned below.

Notice if the block design worked the way you wanted. If not, was the problem simply in the selection of the block, or was it in the way the blocks were put together? Did you use an even number of blocks, horizontally, when an uneven number would have been better?

Did you put a border on the quilt? If so, does it relate well to the design? Does it provide unity and closure? Or does the border take interest away from the body of the quilt by introducing a new idea, color, fabric, shape, or pattern? Is the border's size compatible with the design? Are the shapes in the border in proportion to the rest of the quilt? Is the border in proportion to the total design?

Have you used fabrics that are distracting or that cause disunity? Does any fabric "pull out" from the others? Has your design enough value contrast to clearly see what your design intentions were? Does your design exhibit too much unity, so that it lacks interest or excitement? Or does your design have too much going on, so that there is no pattern, harmony, or unity? Has your quilting line provided the texture needed to enhance your design?

After you have determined the problem, be careful not to repeat it in future projects. If you notice this is a recurring problem, be especially attentive to breaking this detrimental design habit.

2. Designing and Creating a New Quilt

Design a quilt, using the ideas described in this book to help formulate your design plan. Make certain that your chosen block will elicit the type of design you wish by playing with paper blocks first. Decide how many blocks you will need for the best design format. To seek interesting and appropriate border application, cut some of your play blocks apart; play with their arrangement until you have a good idea of what you might want to do.

Attempt to visualize your quilt as much as you can. Visualize its color, fabric, and finished state. Set out the fabrics you plan to include. Formulate a color-fabric plan, so you know in which direction you are headed.

Remember that a design plan for your quilt is not a rigid demand; it is simply a guideline for focus and direction. The plan may work perfectly for you, with few changes made during the construction. However, it is also quite possible that new ideas will evolve as you begin, and you will be excited to try them. Almost always, the better decision is to go with your spirit and intuition if your plan seems too static or uninteresting.

(continued on next page)

Take special precaution, if you set your plan aside to work extemporaneously. This style of working doesn't mean that you cast aside good design application. It simply means you are working from a mental plan, rather than a prearranged paper plan. Regardless of which way you work, it behooves you to work within the design guidelines. If you dismantle your plan for happenstance design, your efforts will probably be disappointing.

A design plan does include determining general overall color and fabric use. However, this does not mean you must determine each shape's color or fabric selection at this stage of work. In the quilt field, most of us work best making fabric choices as we construct. We need to be physically involved with our fabrics as we make fabric decisions. Few of us are satisfied with our paper color plans, as they never seem to capture the ideas we envision. It seems almost impossible to translate on paper the qualities present in fabric.

3. Creating a Medallion Quilt

Challenge yourself to design and create a small medallion quilt. Before planning, reread the information in this chapter so you are clear as to the overall relationship between the body of the quilt and the borders. Take time to plan a quilt that will successfully blend together the different elements within your design. Make certain your central medallion design is interesting and visually strong. Plan your borders carefully, reiterating elements from the central design. Make certain your design shows repetition of color, fabric, shapes, and pattern. This will bring harmony and unity. Also, make certain there is contrast bringing interest to the design. Keep the different shapes in proportion to one another.

4. Planning a Round-Robin Quilt

Forming your own round-robin quilt group allows you to obtain a friendship medallion quilt while you gain experience working on different quilts. It should be an enjoyable experience if your group takes the time to plan wisely. Choose friends whose work (technique and fabric presentation) you admire. Limit your group to a small size, so your group's quilts will not have the severe problem of too many borders dwarfing a center block. An uneven number usually makes a better presentation than an even one. Also, consider the following:

Reread the information in this chapter concerning borders, medallion quilts, and round-robin quilts. Review the design ideas presented in Chapters 2-8. Meet with your group. Take time to discuss the important design characteristics that make a quilt successful. Do not let design play a minor role in your group's planning.

Make certain that each quilter realizes her major creative effort should go into her own quilt's center block, as that sets the stage for the border play thereafter. Everyone's job is so much easier when there is a great center block with which to work. Consider having each quilter set her own basic ground rules for her own quilt design. Otherwise, haphazard design can easily result.

Each group member should understand that each border must relate to the center design. There must be reiteration of elements. Be certain that everyone understands unity and contrast and how to attain both. Discuss the role of the final border.

Set aside time to design the center medallion block before beginning the construction schedule. Don't think of this as insignificant time. Since everything must revolve around the medallion design, each person needs time to think about what she wants to do for her center design. There is no rule that says you must only use one block. You may choose to incorporate two blocks or a wide variety of design motifs that make a fantastic central statement.

After the center designs have been planned, meet again. Then determine the order of rotation, time schedule, and any other details that need to be worked out. Give yourselves realistic goals for finishing each set of borders. Have a party to celebrate the finishing and presentation of the quilts.

Creating traditional block patterns has always been an enjoyable pastime for me. Therefore, I was particularly interested in making new patterns to include in *The Visual Dance—Creating Spectacular Quilts*. I hope you will use many of these designs to work through the concepts presented in this book.

While working on these patterns, it was my primary intent to emphasize designs that could appear layered—patterns with dimensional qualities. I also wanted to design blocks that had great potential for color and design play throughout the quilt's surface. Additionally, most of these blocks have good interlocking capabilities with surrounding blocks. Although some designs are suitable for the experienced beginner, it was my intention to create patterns that would intrigue and excite the intermediate and advanced quiltmaker.

Use your own color interpretation. Include numerous color and fabric changes to achieve a design's greatest potential. Each design has many color possibilities or variations. Our palette was limited for these designs; allow yourself more freedom in your color play than was possible here in print.

I hope you will enjoy working with these new traditional block patterns. They are really a gift to you, my friends and fellow quiltmakers. Have a great time playing with these designs. A pattern drafting review is in *The Magical Effects of Color* (pages 120-123; see Sources). Naturally, I would love to see your completed quilts. So, please send me photos or slides of your finished work.

Enjoy!

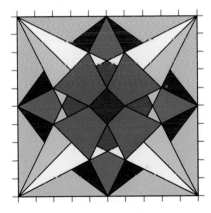

Gem Flower
(©1994 Joen Wolfrom)
Five-patch Pattern
10 x 10 divisions
100-square grid

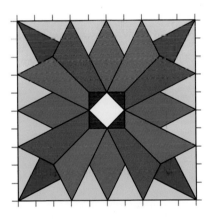

Spring Anenome
(©1994 Joen Wolfrom)
Five-patch Pattern
10 x 10 divisions
100-square grid

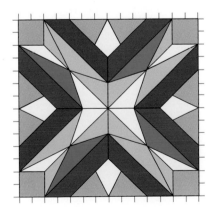

Hidden Star
(©1994 Joen Wolfrom)
Seven-patch Pattern
14 x 14 divisions
196-square grid

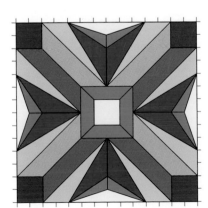

Through the Looking Glass
(©1994 Joen Wolfrom)
Seven-patch Pattern
14 x 14 divisions
196-square grid

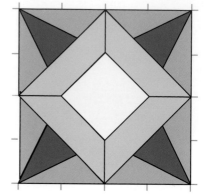

Rolling Square
(©1994 Joen Wolfrom)
Four-patch Pattern
4 x 4 divisions
16-square grid

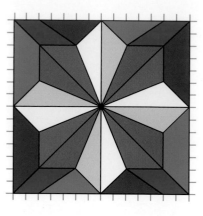

Icelandic Poppy
(©1994 Joen Wolfrom)
Seven-patch Pattern
14 x 14 divisions
196-square grid

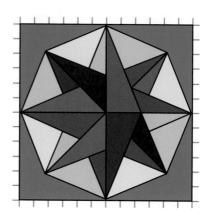

Puzzling Star
(©1994 Joen Wolfrom)
Nine-patch Pattern
12 x 12 divisions
144-square grid

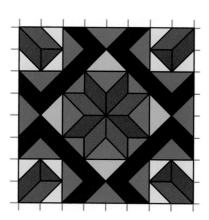

Wedding Ring Glow
(©1994 Joen Wolfrom)
Nine-patch Pattern
6 x 6 divisions
36-square grid

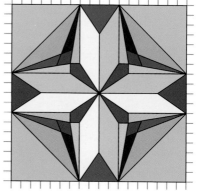

Cutting Edge
(©1994 Joen Wolfrom)
Nine-patch Pattern
18 x 18 divisions
324-square grid

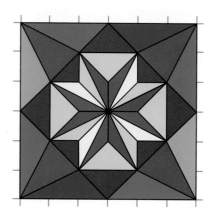

Star Flower Lattice
(©1992 Joen Wolfrom)
Four-patch Pattern
8 x 8 divisions
64-square grid

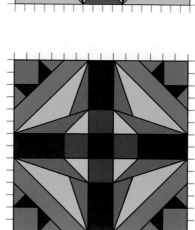

Reflecting Ducks
(©1994 Joen Wolfrom)
Seven-patch Pattern
14 x 14 divisions
196-square grid

A Closing Exhibition of Quilts

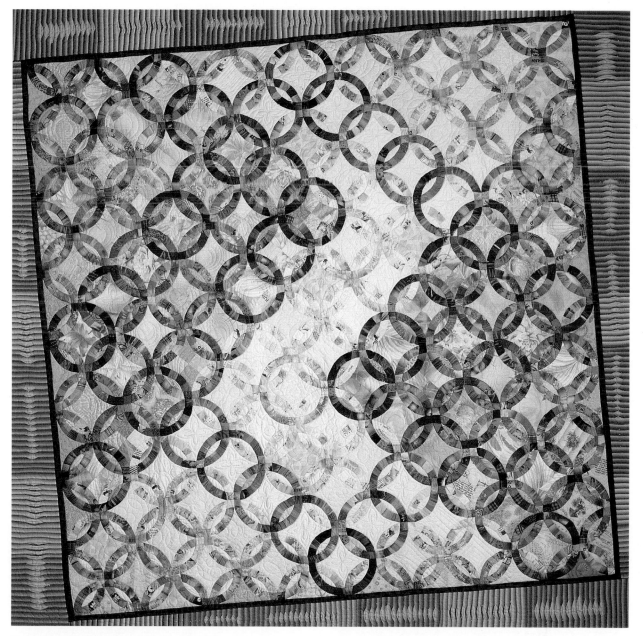

124. SAZANAMI (WATER RING), 1991, 86" x 86"
Junko Sawada, Yokohama-shi, Japan
Junko Sawada creates exquisite quilts through beautiful color sense and intuitive design style. She often uses traditional patterns as her initial inspiration. This quilt, based on the Double Wedding Ring pattern, brings to Junko's mind the illusion of the azure and purple hydrangeas reflected in a pool of water under a rainy gray sky in June. As she worked, Junko pictured the mirrored image of hydrangeas metamorphosed into colorful water rings by sudden raindrops. Junko's border application gives contrast to the design, while it repeats the subtle grayed-blue coloration found in the inner design. Hand-pieced and hand-quilted. Photo: Carina Woolrich

125. STELLAR TRANSFORMATIONS
1989, 68" x 80"
Judy B. Dales, Boonton, New Jersey
Judy's use of rich fabrics and her intuitive color sense blend together to create a beautiful and intriguing positive/negative value study quilt. The design flows from dark figures on a light background to the opposite. Photo: Courtesy of the artist

126. HEAT WAVE, 1993, 63" x 63"
Gloria Hansen, Hightstown, New Jersey
Gloria wanted the challenge of attempting to create heat and energy while using a cool setting in this original design. Machine-pieced and hand-quilted. Photo: Courtesy of the artist

127. NOT QUITE BLACK AND WHITE,
1988, 83" x 83"
Wendy Richardson, Brooklyn Park, Minnesota
The traditional block Joseph's Coat has been visually changed by Wendy's innovative color choices. Photo: Dan Kahler

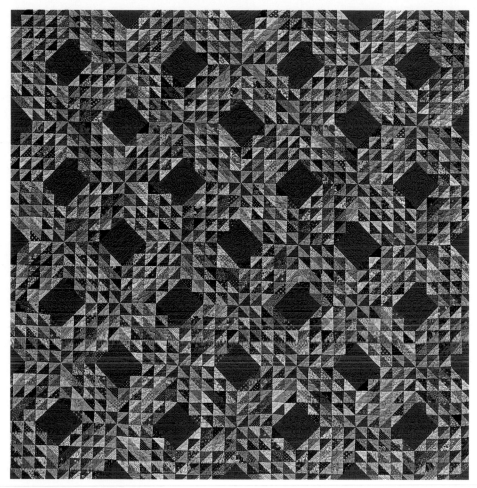

128. BLUE OCEAN WAVES, 1986, 80" x 80"
Marie Goyette Fritz, San Diego, California
The blocks for this friendship quilt were
made by Marie and seven of her friends.
Marie then pieced the blocks together to
create this beautiful example of a tradi-
tional Occan Wave quilt. Hand-quilted.
Photo: Ken Wagner

129. BYZANTINE STAR, 1992, 88" x 101"
Ginny Baird, Scottsdale, Arizona
This beautiful quilt, created by Ginny,
was begun after she saw the pattern in
Angle Antics by Mary Hickey. The
strongly contrasting values make this
quilt particularly striking. Photo: Ken
Wagner

131. SPARKLING STARS AT SEA, 1994, 35" x 35"
Joan Dyer, Redondo Beach, California
Using the Storm at Sea block as her inspiration, Joan has changed the pattern considerably, as she made her fabric and color selections. Her innovative design play created a delightful small quilt. Hand-dyed fabrics, plaids, and prints were used. Photo: Ken Wagner

130. GENESIS, 1993, 67" x 74"
Sylvia Zeveloff, New York, New York
Using color, value, and print fabrics, Sylvia used the sweeping undulations of Storm at Sea to create a scene. She planned the flowers to be dark at the bottom of the quilt where the sunlight did not reach. As the flowers move toward the sunlit sky, they appear lighter. The sky moves gradually from the lightness of day into its evening stages, eventually ending at darkness. Photo: Jack Ward, New York

132. SOUTHWEST HIDDEN WELLS, 1993, 83" x 103"
Lois W. Horton, Sun City West, Arizona
This quilt was created from only one piece of fabric: a striped VIP screen print. Using a large variety of rectangular shapes, Lois cut and sewed the stripes together to create this design. Hidden Wells pattern by Mary Ellen Hopkins. Free-motion machine quilting by Stephanie Cornet. Photo: Ken Wagner

133. HOW DOES YOUR GARDEN GROW?, 1992, 64" x 73"
Laura Heine, Billings, Montana
This wonderful, unique garden quilt is innovatively constructed by strip-piecing and latticework. Laura has dyed, overdyed, and bleached some of the print fabrics to obtain the subtle gradations she needed for her vision. Machine-quilted with stippling. Photo: Daniel Tilton, Montana

134. WHAT STAR IS THIS?, 1993, 32" x 37"
Shawn Walker Levy, Trumbauersville, Pennsylvania
Using the traditional blocks Evening Star, Windmill, Clay's Choice, and Fancy Stripe, this design uses the concept of exaggeration to create its focus. Photo: Ken Wagner

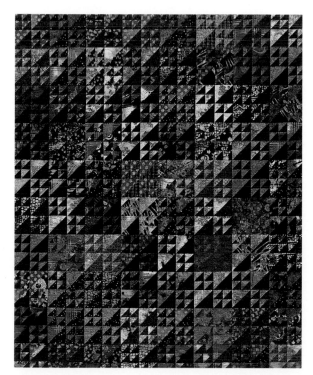

135. GEESE MUST BE BRIGHT IF THEY CHOOSE TO FLY AT NIGHT, 1992, 67" x 83"
Kari Lane, Lansing, Kansas
Kari chose bold colors for her spirited quilt using the traditional block pattern Flock (Flock of Geese). Using black as a visual stabilizer in her multi-colored design, Kari has captured a feeling of excitement and happiness. Photo: Ken Wagner

136. SAY IT WITH FLOWERS, 1994, 23" x 29"
Sylvia Kundrats, Quakertown, Pennsylvania
Dozens of print fabrics were cut into 2" squares to create this floral picture. Sylvia used both sides of many fabrics to achieve a background and foregound that reflected a light source falling on an object. Inspired by the works of Deirdre Amsden, the pioneer of this technique (see Sources), Pat Magaret, and Donna Slusser. Photo: Ken Wagner

137. MONTEREY BAY, 1988, 68" x 85"
Judy Mathieson, Woodland Hills, California
This gorgeous quilt is one in a series of Attic Window quilts created by Judy. The three print fabrics used
to create this scene represent the marine ecology and cypress trees for which Monterey Bay is famous. The
uniquely latticed window framing and border application work marvelously with the scenic design. Photo:
Courtesy of the artist

Bibliography

Bevlin, Marjorie Elliott. *Design Through Discovery: The Elements and Principles*. New York, NY: Holt Rinehart Winston, 1985.

Beyer, Jinny. *The Quilter's Album of Blocks & Borders*. McLean, VA: EPM Publications, Inc., 1980.

Lauer, David. *Design Basics*. San Francisco, CA: Holt, Rinehart and Winston, 1990.

Malone, Maggie. *1001 Patchwork Designs*. New York, NY: Sterling Publishing Co., Inc., 1982.

Mills, Susan Winter. *849 Traditional Patchwork Patterns*. New York, NY: Dover Publications, Inc., 1989.

Rising, Gerald R., William T. Bailey, Stephen I. Brown, John A. Graham, and Alice M. King. *Unified Mathematics, Book 2*. Palo Alto, CA: Houghton Mifflin, 1985.

Editorial Advice of Chicago University Faculty. *Compton's Encyclopedia*. Chicago, IL: Compton's Learning Company, 1986.

Sources

PATTERNS:

Pieced picture patterns of original designs by Cynthia England are available. For a brochure send LSASE (Large self-addressed, stamped envelope) to England Design Studios, 803 Voyager, Houston, Texas 77062.

The pattern for *The Other Side of My Grandmother's Flower Garden* (photo 62) and other original designs by Jane Kakaley are available. For inquiries, send a LSASE to: Jane Kakaley, 12255 SE 56th Street, #312, Bellevue, Washington 98006.

FABRIC:

Skydyes (hand painted) from Mickey Lawler, 83 Richmond Lane, West Hartford, CT 06117

Lunn Fabrics from Debra Lunn & Michael Mrowka, 357 Santa Fe Drive, Denver, Colorado 80223 (303-623-2710)

GENERAL QUILTING SUPPLIES BY MAIL ORDER:

Quilts & Other Comforts, P.O. Box 4101, Golden, Colorado 80402-4101. (Phone: 303-278-1010)

SUGGESTED RESOURCE BOOKS FOR YOUR PERSONAL LIBRARY:

It is a difficult task to decide what to purchase for our personal quilt library, as the selection is often overwhelming. I have compiled a small list of books that include some of my all-time favorite quilting books, as well as new ones that I eagerly invite into my collection. These are a sampling of the many books available in our field. Read and enjoy.

Appliqué 12 Easy Ways by Elly Sienkiewicz

Baltimore Beauties and Beyond, Volume 1 by Elly Sienkiewicz

Celtic Spirals by Philomena Durcan (Self-published: 834 W. Remington Drive, Sunnyvale, CA 94087)

Colourwash Quilts by Deirdre Amsden

Dimensional Appliqué by Elly Sienkiewicz

Encyclopedia of Pieced Quilt Patterns compiled by Barbara Brackman

Incredible Quilts for Kids of All Ages by Jean Ray Laury

Lessons in Machine Piecing by Marsha McCloskey

Quilter's Complete Guide by Marianne Fons and Liz Porter

Perfect Pineapples by Jane Hall and Dixie Haywood

Pieced Borders: The Complete Resource by Judy Martin and Marsha McCloskey

Precision Pieced Quilts Using the Foundation Method by Jane Hall and Dixie Haywood

Sewing on the Line by Lesly-Claire Greenberg

The Art of Silk Ribbon Embroidery by Judith Baker Montano

Strips That Sizzle by Margaret Miller

Watercolor Quilts by Pat Magaret and Donna Slusser

OTHER BOOKS BY JOEN WOLFROM:

Landscapes & Illusions: Creating Scenic Imagery With Fabric

The Magical Effects of Color

Other Fine Quilting Books are available from C&T Publishing. Write or call:
C&T Publishing, P.O. Box 1456, Lafayette, California 94549 (1-800-284-1114)

Joen began quiltmaking in 1974 after she left her career in the educational field to become a homemaker. Her interest in color, design, and contemporary quilt art surfaced in the early 1980s. During that time, Joen challenged herself to experiment with new techniques and visual ideas. She is noted for being the innovator of several techniques, including strip-pieced landscapes and organic curved designs. She is the innovator of the *free-form freezer paper technique*, which is often used in curved and straight-line piecing. Her work is included in collections throughout the world.

Joen has taught and lectured in the quilting field both nationally and internationally since 1984. Additionally, she has been invited to jury and judge several national quilt shows. Previously published books are *Landscapes &*
Illusions: Creating Scenic Imagery with Fabric and *The Magical Effects of Color*.

Joen's other interests include gardening and landscape design, playing bridge, reading, and spending quiet times with friends and family. When not travelling, Joen enjoys the private quietness of her family's home in a rural setting on a small island in Washington State. There she enjoys life with her three children and husband—Danielle, Dane, David, and Dan.

Inquiries about workshop and lecture bookings and other correspondence may be sent directly to Joen Wolfrom at 104 Bon Bluff, Fox Island, Washington 98333. Requests for a current teaching schedule may be sent to the same address (include a large self-addressed, stamped envelope).

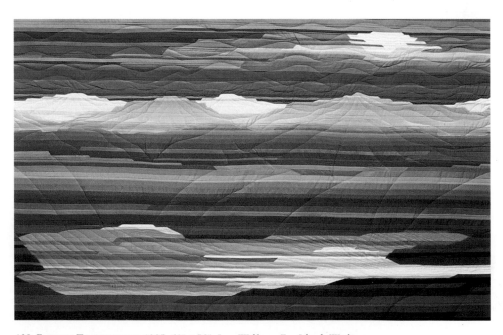

138. EVENING TRANQUILLITY, 1985, 60" x 38", *Joen Wolfrom, Fox Island, Washington*